THE 6% LIFE

7 Strategies That Successful Entrepreneurs Use to Reengineer Their Life to Consistently Pay Less Than 6% in Taxes

SHAUNA A. WEKHERLIEN, CPA
MTAX, CTC, CTS, TAX GODDESS

THE 6% LIFE

7 Strategies That Successful Entrepreneurs Use to Reengineer Their Life to Consistently Pay Less Than 6% in Taxes

Copyright © 2023. Tax Goddess Publishing, LLC.

All rights reserved. No part of this publication may be reproduced, distributed, or transmitted in any form or by any means, including photocopying, recording, or other electronic or mechanical methods, without the prior written permission of the copyright holder, except in the case of brief quotations embodied in critical reviews and certain other noncommercial uses permitted by copyright law.

TAX GODDESS® Publishing

ISBN: 978-0-9960329-1-9

The publisher and the author do not make any guarantee or other promise as to any results that may be obtained from using the content of this book. You should never make any financial decision without first consulting with your own advisor and conducting your own research and due diligence. To the maximum extent permitted by law, the publisher and the author disclaim any and all liability in the event any information, commentary, analysis, opinions, advice and/or recommendations contained in this book prove to be inaccurate, incomplete or unreliable, or result in any investment or other losses. The publisher and author make no guarantees concerning the level of success you may experience by following the advice and strategies contained in this book, and you accept the risk that results will differ for each individual.

Printed in the United States of America.

> In this world nothing can be said to be certain, except death and taxes.
> —Benjamin Franklin

CONTENTS

CONNECT WITH SHAUNA xi

PART I: INTRODUCTION: WHAT IS THE 6% LIFE? .. 1

    Chairs Flying, a Goddess Born 3

    Navigating Your Financial Journey (Ignore Only If You Hate Money) 15

    Who Is Shauna, the Tax Goddess (and Why Should We Listen to Her)? 18

    Who This Book Is For 21

    Unmasking the Myth: Are Tax Strategies Really Just for the Rich? 24

    Buckle up for the Adventure—Taxes Have Never Been This Fun! 27

    Charting Your Course— Understanding the Aggression Scale 29

PART II: STRATEGIES FOR THE 6% LIFE 31

    A Good Tax Plan Is Always Free 33

        The Strategy: Captive Insurance for Business Owners 35

        The Implementation 44

        The Pitfalls 47

        Extreme Cases That Will Get You Thrown in Jail 50

        If You Want to Know More (BONUS) 52

- Kids—Just Cute? No, a Supreme Tax Advantage...........55
  - The Strategy: Paying Your Children 100% Tax-Free .57
  - The Implementation 67
  - The Pitfalls..70
  - Extreme Cases That Will Get You Thrown in Jail......72
  - If You Want to Know More (BONUS).......................74
- Massively Fund Your Retirement, Even if You Are Way Behind the Eight Ball—Two Heads Are Better than One 77
  - The Strategy: Defined Benefit, Cash Balance, and 401(k) Programs 79
  - The Implementation 88
  - The Pitfalls..92
  - Extreme Cases That Will Get You Thrown in Jail......95
  - If You Want to Know More (BONUS).......................97
- Selling Without Taxation: Keep ALL Your Money........99
  - The Strategy: Section 453 and DSTs 101
  - The Implementation 107
  - The Pitfalls..110
  - Extreme Cases That Will Get You Thrown in Jail....112
  - If You Want to Know More (BONUS).....................114

The $190,000 "Oopsie" 115
    The Strategy: Proper Use of an Accountable Plan 117
    The Implementation 129
    The Pitfalls 133
    Extreme Cases That Will Get You Thrown in Jail ... 136
    If You Want to Know More (BONUS) 138
Time Is Money, Money Is Time 141
    The Strategy: Infinite Banking & Premium
    Financing 143
    The Implementation 151
    The Pitfalls 154
    Extreme Cases That Will Get You Thrown in Jail ... 157
    If You Want to Know More (BONUS) 159
$175k Tax-Free Every Year 161
    The Strategy: The Masters Exemption (AKA The
    Augusta Rule) 163
    The Implementation 169
    The Pitfalls 172
    Extreme Cases That Will Get You Thrown in Jail ... 174
    If You Want to Know More (BONUS) 177
Tying It All Together 179

PART III: HOW TO GET EVEN MORE HELP 181

Your Golden Ticket to The 6% Life 183
How to Access Your Bonuses 185
Speak to Us 187
Acknowledgments 189
About the Author 191

Dedication

To my mother—my eternal beacon, my goddess whose strength and wisdom continue to guide me through the journey of life.

And to the remarkable and indefatigable team at Tax Goddess, whose unwavering support has transformed mere ideas into vivid realities, turning my dreams into tangible success. This book is a testament to your faith, perseverance, and relentless pursuit of excellence.

CONNECT WITH SHAUNA

FACEBOOK

YOUTUBE

INSTAGRAM

TWITTER

LINKEDIN

I can't wait to meet each and every one of you!

Shauna~

PART I

INTRODUCTION

WHAT IS THE 6% LIFE?

Chairs Flying, a Goddess Born

When a chair flew across the room, my eyes grew big. I had NEVER seen that type of reaction from my mother...

When you see a chair fly across the room, it can be terrifying, especially if it's the first time you've ever seen your mother upset.

What could have taken this very stoic woman who had always prided herself on maintaining her calm, cool, and class and turned her into this enraged woman I had never seen before in my entire life?

You see, I was a daughter in a family business. I was 18, beginning college, preparing for a life in my dream career—astrophysics. Mom, a single mother, owned a construction business and worked many long days, grueling hours, providing for my younger sister and me.

This year, she had had a very successful year in her construction business. Over the past year, she was always so excited, talking about moving on to build her dream project—building custom homes—building what she wanted to create and not what she had to build to satisfy others. Finally, she could take her vision and make it a reality. A chance to make "art" instead of just building a thing. She had worked for her clients' dreams for years. She was doing boring projects, making money for others, working long hours, and grinding away her nights. She wanted freedom. She wanted to build a life for herself and my sister and me where she could control the outcome, the product, and the dream. She kept talking about how she would use the money she had been slaving away to earn to fund this new venture. Mom and I were heading on our dream paths, and nothing could be better.

We were sitting at the kitchen table on a regular Sunday morning. Mom was drinking her coffee and reviewing her onion skin architectural diagrams on the table. The birds were chirping; the sky was a beautiful blue with no clouds in sight. I was rereading one of my favorite books, *Cosmos* by Carl Sagan (yes, I know, I'm a complete science nerd, LOL). I glanced at my mom, and she had the biggest smile on her face.

"This is going to be amazing. I can't wait to get started once the permits are approved."

I smiled. It was lovely to see her so happy and content with her world. I adore my mom, so seeing her beam at the prospect of starting her new project made me feel peaceful.

"Well, enough dreaming for today. I had better get to work," Mom said as she stood up from the table to grab the mail from the kitchen counter that had come in that day. She picked up several envelopes and a few larger packages and brought them to the table to start sorting them. A few pieces of trash and some pieces of random junk mail went into the trash bin as she was sorting.

As I watched her, thinking about how proud I am to be the daughter of this extraordinary woman, I saw her face sink.

"Mom? What's that?" I asked as I saw her staring at an unopened envelope.

"It's from the IRS ..." she said as she started to open the letter and read what it said.

Suddenly, Mom slammed her fists on the kitchen table and threw her chair backward violently as she stood up in frustration. I could see her anger, disbelief, resentment, and defeat.

"I can't believe that they want MORE money! This is ridiculous! There has to be something I can do ..." she mumbled in a half-broken tone.

"What?! What do you mean?" I asked.

Mom calmed down pretty quickly. She pulled the chair back over to the table, sat down, took a deep breath, and looked at me. She was so serious. All the joy from 10 minutes ago was gone entirely.

"The government wants more money. I just can't believe it. I've taken every tax break that I can think of. I've spoken with my CPA, and we've tried to strategize. Although I believe we've done a good job, the government still wants more. It's ridiculous to think that all of my hard-earned money must be sent to the government rather than caring for you and your sister."

She was on the verge of tears. A state I had never seen her in.

My heart sank.

According to the notice, Mom was forced to give up 50% of her income to the government. The worst part was that she realized she wouldn't be able to start her dream project. She was devastated.

I desperately wanted to do anything I could to help her. I mean, come on, this was the woman I had looked up to all of my life. To see her this upset was heart-wrenching. Especially over what I thought should be a pretty simple problem for her team of tax and finance experts. Lowering taxes was their entire job, right? Had they tried everything? Had they put in the effort? Were they even trained in strategies (versus just how to prepare taxes)? Usually, this woman could figure out an answer to absolutely anything. I knew there had to be a better way, some strategies I could learn or information I could obtain. I know that she had some top-notch CPAs, so why weren't they doing anything about this? There had to be something that was missed on her behalf.

I started reading anything and everything that I could get my hands on to learn more about taxes. I knew there had to be a better option other than Mom simply handing over her hard-earned money to the government. There must be something else she could do.

I found articles during my reading and research describing wealthy entrepreneurs who effectively paid nothing in taxes. Eureka! If they could do it, so could we. If I was going to figure out how they did that, I had to start somewhere. My university had accounting and tax-specific classes. I loved astrophysics, but I loved my mother more. So I went to the admissions office and changed my major to accounting and finance the next day.

I dove into it. I decided to become one of the top tax strategists in the world. My reading tripled; I began hunting for mentors and searching for any tip, trick, or tool I could use to help my family. There had to be someone or something that could help me get to where I wanted to go.

Then, I found her. Dominique.

Dominique was the head of an organization out of California called Certified Tax Coach, CTC. She was speaking at a specialty conference for tax CPAs on tax strategies for business owners, new tax strategies, and ways to look at the world that are different from what normal CPAs do.

The conference was life-changing. Dominique triggered in my mind a giant game of chess. How to play within the rules of the Tax Code, moving the pieces to reach your goals.

I knew this was the path I needed to follow to get what I wanted.

Dominique's program was the beginning stepping stone to the creation of The 6% Life.

My goal was to reduce my mother's taxes to the bare legal minimum required. I was going to gain the education, experience, and knowledge of the application of tax strategies and reduction techniques. I wanted Mom to be able to build her dream projects, her custom homes. I wanted her to be able to use her cash for what she deemed essential in her life: taking care of her family, my little sister, and me.

The tax strategies I was looking for existed in the world (normally held in secret for the elite and ultra-wealthy). I was going to bring the strategies to the "little guy" like my mom and the entrepreneurs and business owners who worked tirelessly every day, 12+ hours a day, day in, day out, working their hands to the bone. Dying inside because they had to hand most of their money to the government when they knew they could do so much more for their families and community than the government ever could or would.

After the conference, I became obsessed. I wouldn't let up as I hunted down the best strategies I could get my hands on. I reached out to every top-tier tax strategist, advisor, CPA, knowledgeable professional, and partner with tax strategies that could assist me. Anyone that would talk to me.

"So, how have you been?"

"Good. Focused. You know my goal. I've got to get this tax payment down. The government is just insane. Taxing the business owners who build and grow this country ..."

Alex and I had been friends for a few years now. He was my mentor. Older, wiser, and driven, just like me. We always got along well. We were eating lunch and discussing my frustrations with trying to get the answers I was looking for.

Laughingly, Alex said, "Well, what do you expect? Most CPAs

don't really care about their clients. They only care about making it easy for themselves, earning more money, churn and burn. Many of them focus on how to get more returns in the door, get that cash, and retire sooner. They don't want to work with clients on the details; they don't want to dig and search to save their clients money. Clients have been so well trained to just hand their money over to the government, so why would any CPA choose to work hard?"

"Because it's ridiculous," I said, exasperated. "I can't believe that clients just accept this as a matter of fact. Are they not reading and seeing the same articles that I am? Multibillionaires are not paying a single penny in tax. So how can they not think to themselves, 'Why can't I do that?'"

"Listen, clients do whatever the CPA tells them to do. And if the CPAs are not proactive, not searching for strategies, and not providing guidance, the clients just accept it. I know you have your own reasons, and that's why I love working with you. Keep on your path. The strategies are out there, and if anyone's going to find them, it's you."

Alex knew me too well. He knew I wouldn't drop this. Not when it came to my mother, my family.

I left that lunch even more determined to find the answers. I couldn't believe what I was hearing from Alex, but it was what I had seen. CPAs saying it was "OK" to take money away from hard-working families across the country because they couldn't be bothered to put in the time, energy, and effort to find options to reduce their clients' taxes.

I was appalled, furious, and feeling heavy-hearted. Here I was, training to be a CPA, but I certainly didn't want to be like those "basic" CPAs that just wanted to churn and burn clients, make money, and retire. I wanted to help people like my mother. Hard-working, honest business owners who were trying to do the best for their families. How could any CPA sleep at night knowing what they were letting happen to these entrepreneurs, the backbone of our country?! My mom's happiness and ability to pursue her dreams were worth so much more to me than money ever could be.

Now, if you've ever met me, you know me. I am a redhead with a very driven personality. Nothing was getting in my way. I was going to help Mom if it was the last thing I did.

The time came. I was ready to show Mom the plan.

"Hey, Mom," I said into the phone. "Can we sit down for an extra hour on Sunday this week? I've got something to show you."

"Of course, sweetie. See you then."

When she hung up the phone, I was both excited and nervous. I was about to show her The 6% Life tax plan I had customized for her.

Mom was so proud of me for changing majors and going into taxes. She was pleased to see what I was trying to accomplish. She kept telling her friends how smart and talented her daughter was. (And I totally accepted the bragging!) I had the perfect plan and couldn't wait to show her. It was flawless!

That Sunday, we sat down at that same kitchen table with all my charts and tables. I pulled out the big guns, describing every strategy and option in detail. I showed her how the techniques worked together to get her down to a 6% tax bill.

"Oh, sweetie." I knew that tone of voice and my heart sank ... "This is great, and you've done a good job putting it all together. I can see the hard work. But honey, there's no way you can get me down to 6% on the tax burden. I've had teams of experts look at this stuff. They haven't been able to figure it out. I know you're smart, but some of these sound a little sketchy. You're not trying to get your mom thrown into jail, are you?" she said sweetly, kindly, and laughingly.

I was devastated!

"Of course not, Mom. These are real strategies. The big guys use them. Have your CPAs ever brought you these as ideas? Honestly, from everything I can see that they've done on your files, they haven't brought any of these to your attention." She listened with that mother-knows-best smile on her face.

"Mom, I can do this because I care about you and what happens to you, and I love seeing you smile. I have pulled every lever, tactic, and strategy over the years of study to develop this plan for you. The other professionals you've worked with don't care about you. I've studied with these people and gone to conferences with them. They only care about themselves and the money they can make, with no stress/no work for them. They care about getting as many clients in and out the door as possible. You are MY mother. You are the reason I am doing this. You are why I switched from astrophysics to tax. I am doing this because I want to help you. I built this for you."

Her face changed. She stared at me, a little shocked and wide-eyed. Her eyes became teary.

She said, "And, you are sure? This will work?"

"Yes, Mom. I've got you. This will work."

Mom agreed, and we implemented the strategies. As a result, she legally paid only 6% in taxes that year.

And that same year, she built her first custom home, her dream, her art come to life. Her soul was free.

From then on, I decided to use these powers for good. I employed these same tax strategies to help friends, family, and, eventually, clients reach the same results—The 6% Life.

So, Mom was covered; she was now living The 6% Life. Paying the taxes required of her, but not a penny more.

I became a red-headed, fire-breathing, tax-saving dragon. I sat on top of a pile of golden tax strategies. Each gold piece was another one I could initiate and implement for any client.

I've had many favorite moments over the years being a USA Top 1% tax strategist. Besides helping Mom, I think my favorite moment was when I delivered an STC (Strategic Tax Coaching) plan to a crying mother.

I wish I could say she was crying because of how much money

we saved her, but she was crying because she found out her five-year-old son had cancer and needed a $50,000 surgery that she could not afford.

Working with her and her business, applying our 6% Life strategies, we found her over $80,000 of tax savings—money she did not need to send to the government. At the end of our delivery meeting, she cried tears of joy instead of sadness. We helped her pay for her son's cancer surgery. One of the most impactful moments of my life—what could be better?! This was yet another moment telling me that this path is what I need to do for the world. This message and knowledge had to be spread.

So, we come back to my mother. It had been a while since she received that IRS notice, and it had been a long time since she had overpaid her taxes. Being a 6% Lifer made her dreams come true. Her first custom home dream project was a massive success, one I got to drive past every day on my way to the office, thinking of her. She can build and live free to create her art in her custom homes. My heart couldn't sing any louder.

Since beginning this journey, I've been able to help over 4,200 entrepreneurs, their families, and their businesses. They've massively improved their cash flow, reduced their taxes, and, most importantly, achieved their hopes, dreams, and goals. They are keeping their money with them—the only appropriate place for it. My 6% Life clients have been able to buy the rental properties they want for retirement. Build their retirement portfolios. Pay for their kids' college. Pay for their mom's medical bills and buy her a house of her own. They have been able to buy that dream boat they have wanted since they were a child. They've traveled around the world and had the business pay for it. They've paid for their kids' cancer surgery.

I couldn't ask for a life more rewarding than seeing the smile on their faces when their dreams become a reality. Things they never thought they could have are now in their hands. I feel proud and honored to serve when I deliver a tax plan and get a client to The 6% (or less!) Life.

The successes I've created for clients led me to build my company, Tax Goddess, into a specialized tax reduction strategy CPA firm. Our sole mission is to reduce the taxes that business owners and entrepreneurs pay the government, so they can keep their cash and do with it as they wish.

This experience has taught me to go after what I want and you should do the same thing. Go after your dreams and goals. Help those around you that you feel are most important to help. These are the things that give you the drive and passion for doing what you want to do in life. If it doesn't exist, then build it.

Navigating Your Financial Journey (Ignore Only If You Hate Money)

Just imagine you're in a boat on a vast ocean, armed with only a compass and the stars to guide you. The waters you're navigating are deep, mysterious, and unpredictable. At times, you'll enjoy calm seas and clear skies; at others, you might encounter stormy weather and turbulent waves. This ocean is your financial journey.

As a business owner, you've already set sail. Your boat is your business, the compass is this book, and the stars are your financial goals.

You're already making impressive waves, with a gross income of over $1 million per year. But, as any experienced sailor knows, earning more doesn't necessarily equate to smoother sailing. In fact, the waters may get even more challenging.

Let's consider Paul, an entrepreneur who runs a highly successful tech start-up.

Just a few years ago, he was elated to see his company break the million-dollar revenue mark. It was a dream come true, a testament to his hard work and innovative spirit.

It didn't take long for Paul to realize that higher earnings brought along higher taxes and more complex financial management. The waters he was sailing turned from a tranquil bay into a demanding ocean, seemingly overnight.

This book is your navigational guide. It will help you understand how to ride the waves, whether they're choppy or calm, and navigate through the complexities of your financial journey as a business owner.

The storms may seem daunting, the waves turbulent, but armed with the right knowledge and tools, you're more than capable of steering your boat to the destination of your dreams: financial stability, minimized taxes, and a thriving business, all part of The 6% Life.

This book is filled with stories like Paul's, stories that offer practical lessons derived from real-life scenarios. Each story introduces different tax strategies, business principles, and financial management tips.

As you read each case study, take a moment to reflect on how it relates to your journey. Consider your business practices, your financial strategies, and your overall goals. The situations described in these stories may differ from yours in specifics, but the principles remain the same.

As a sailor, you wouldn't try to cross an ocean without the right navigational tools. Likewise, as a business owner, you should not attempt to navigate your financial journey without a clear understanding of the principles and strategies that will lead you to success.

I want you to engage with these stories, learn from the experiences of others, and start plotting your course.

Remember, sailing an ocean requires constant adjustments. There will be times when you need to change direction, set new goals, or seek expert advice. The team at Tax Goddess is here to support you as you make these adjustments. Don't hesitate to reach out to us when you're ready to take the next step.

In the following chapters, we'll delve deeper into the specifics of these strategies, providing you with a detailed roadmap for your journey.

With each story, each piece of advice, and each strategy, you'll gain the knowledge to steer your business ship through the open seas of financial complexity and into the calm bay of The 6% Life.

The journey ahead is an exciting one, so let's set sail.

Who Is Shauna, the Tax Goddess (and Why Should We Listen to Her)?

As dawn breaks, I, Shauna A. Wekherlien, CPA, MTax, CTC, CTS, also known as the Tax Goddess, am already immersed in my passion—the intricate world of tax strategy.

From my vibrant, lush greenery-filled home office, with a cup of steaming tea by my side, I navigate tax codes, investigate recent tax developments, and craft high-level strategies for my clients.

I am not your ordinary Certified Public Accountant.

Rather, I have been hailed as a financial virtuoso, a seasoned explorer charting the labyrinthine terrain of tax laws.

As the founder of Tax Goddess Business Services, a boutique tax and accounting firm, I lead a team of over 89 global professionals who are a massive part of the heart and soul of Tax Goddess and our dedication and service to our clients.

Founded in 2004, we have been diligently helping clients shrink their tax bills for nearly two decades.

My journey into the tax world was seeded early, inspired by my mother, a resolute business owner with an indomitable spirit.

I found joy in deciphering financial puzzles, which later propelled me into the universe of advanced tax strategy—a realm that offered endless challenges and immense gratification.

After graduating from the University of Arizona with an accounting and finance double degree, I became a Certified Public Accountant. Still, I yearned for more.

My quest for deeper knowledge led me to Arizona State University for my Master's in Taxation (MTax) and then to become a Certified Tax Coach (CTC).

Never one to settle, I am now ranked in the top 3 of only 15 professionals nationwide to attain the coveted Certified Tax Strategist (CTS) designation.

Throughout my career, my mission has been to demystify the bewildering world of tax for entrepreneurs and business owners.

I happily transform complex tax jargon into everyday language, helping my clients explore opportunities that a typical CPA might overlook in order to maximize deductions and minimize tax liabilities.

So, why should you listen to me?

The answer is simple—my unrivaled approach to tax strategy.

I am not restricted by traditional tax thinking; instead, I design personalized tax plans that marry each client's personal and business aspirations.

I ardently believe that tax planning is a year-long activity and not just an afterthought during tax season. Whatever you don't do by 12/31 becomes your worst nightmare when it comes to paying the tax bill!

As we journey through this book, be prepared to challenge the norm and learn how I, the Tax Goddess, have saved my clients over a staggering $1 billion. Be ready to revolutionize your financial life, all the while enjoying the experience.

Tax strategy isn't mundane—at least not when you're in the vibrant, trailblazing world of the Tax Goddess.

Who This Book Is For

Welcome to a chapter dedicated to the heart of this book's audience—you. The individuals and businesses ready to turn the tables on their tax strategies and embrace a tax-savvy future.

This book, much like the services we offer at Tax Goddess, isn't for everyone. We've carved out a niche, focusing on certain types of entrepreneurs and business owners. So, who is this book for, exactly?

Firstly, it's for the high-flyers, those businesses that have gross revenues exceeding $1 million per year.

This isn't a small achievement; it signifies your success and the potential for further growth. However, with greater earnings comes more complex tax situations and, naturally, higher tax liabilities.

If this sounds like you, this book is designed to guide you through these complexities and help you strategically reduce your tax liabilities.

Secondly, we have the winners. These are individuals and businesses netting over $300,000 per year.

You're successful, no doubt, but are you maximizing your earnings and minimizing your tax liabilities? If you're keen on growing your wealth and keeping more of what you earn, this book can be your roadmap.

Thirdly, this book is for go-getters paying over $100,000 per year in taxes.

You've worked hard for your money; shouldn't it be working just as hard for you? In this book, you'll find the strategies you need to make your money work smarter, not harder.

Next up, we have the adventurers, those willing to be aggressive but always within the bounds of legality.

Taxes can feel like a burden, but when navigated strategically, they can become a powerful tool for wealth preservation and growth. If you're willing to think outside the box and take calculated risks, this book is for you.

Lastly, this book is for the doers, those ready for action and substantial tax savings.

If you're not afraid of rolling up your sleeves and diving deep into strategic tax planning, then welcome aboard. This book can guide you through the ins and outs of tax planning, helping you realize significant savings.

Our Strategic Tax Coaching (STC) program, which this book mirrors, guarantees a 3X return on investment or your money back. Using our proprietary Tax-o-rithim Formula, we've saved clients over $1 billion in taxes, using strategies that the likes of Musk and Bezos swear by.

If you're ready to transform your tax game and join these ranks, then this book is your starting point. It's time to make your money work smarter, not harder!

Unmasking the Myth: Are Tax Strategies Really Just for the Rich?

"Tax strategies are for the rich. I don't have that kind of money—it's too expensive."

If this sentiment echoes your own, then this chapter is for you. We often hear this objection, and it's not surprising. After all, headlines are filled with stories about the rich and famous using intricate tax strategies to minimize their tax bills, often paying significantly less tax than ordinary folk.

It's easy to assume that these strategies are only accessible to the super-rich. But here's the truth: strategic tax planning is not just for the wealthy; it's for anyone committed to making their money work smarter.

Let's consider the tale of two giants: Amazon and Tesla, both helmed by incredibly wealthy individuals and employing teams of tax experts.

Recent news broke that Amazon, one of the world's most valuable companies, paid zero corporate taxes in 2018 despite recording profits of over $11 billion!

Tesla, on the other hand, went a step further. It not only evaded taxes but also secured a tax rebate of $1.3 billion from the state of Nevada by leveraging tax abatements and credits.

How is this possible?

The answer ... LEGAL STRATEGIC TAX PLANNING. These companies take advantage of every tax law, credit, deduction, and loophole available to them.

Now, think about your business. Could you use a page from their playbook?

Is your CPA bringing strategies to your attention (or are you having to beg for ideas every year with no real positive changes)?

"But wait," you might say. "These companies have billions of dollars and can afford the best tax strategists money can buy. I can't afford that!"

Here's where we challenge this objection. The price tag might seem daunting, but with our guarantee of a 3X return on investment, you can't lose money. Think of it this way: if a service promised you $180,000 in tax savings for a $60,000 investment, would it still be too expensive?

When reframed this way, it's clear that **strategic tax planning isn't an expense; it's an investment**, one that offers substantial returns.

Moreover, remember that doing nothing and choosing NOT to have a tax strategy can be even more expensive!

Every dollar overpaid in taxes is a dollar that could have been invested back into your business, used for personal growth, or saved for future needs.

In conclusion, strategic tax planning isn't about how rich you are, it's about how smart you are with your money. It's about ensuring that every dollar you earn works as hard as you do. So, don't let the myth deter you.

Regardless of your income level, you can utilize strategic tax planning to maximize your wealth, just like the rich and famous.

It's not a matter of affordability; it's a matter of priority. Is keeping more of your hard-earned money a priority for you? If yes, then strategic tax planning is not an option; it's a necessity.

Buckle up for the Adventure—Taxes Have Never Been This Fun!

Welcome to the most electrifying, thrilling, chair-grabbing chapter of your tax journey!

Yeah, yeah, I know … I can almost see the skeptical look on your face. Fun and taxes in the same sentence?

That's like saying "Root canal—the thrilling experience" or "Snakes—the ideal pet." But I'm not joking. Well, except maybe about the snakes.

You see, taxes are like a fantasy novel, filled with strange creatures (tax codes), magic spells (deductions), and hidden treasures (savings).

And just like in those novels, you, the hero, must navigate the labyrinth of laws, understand arcane spells, and discover treasure buried deep within cryptic texts. Sounds daunting, doesn't it? Well, it's about to become the most exciting quest you've ever embarked on.

Do you want to know why taxes are really like a theme park? Because much like roller coasters, they have their ups and downs.

One moment you're soaring high with a profitable quarter, and the next, you're plummeting with a massive tax bill.

But with the right guide (that's us), you'll not only enjoy the ride but also make sure it's mostly "ups."

And the best part?

You won't have to face this adventure alone. We'll be with you every step of the way, equipping you with the knowledge and tools to turn this daunting task into a thrilling journey.

You can find us on YouTube, where we bring tax strategies to life with engaging videos. Sign up for our e-courses to deepen your knowledge at your own pace. Or join our weekly 6% Life Group Coaching program to stay updated with the latest in tax strategy, while also engaging with a community of like-minded adventurers.

So, how about a little humor to get the ball rolling? Here's a classic one for you: Why don't accountants read novels? Because the only numbers in them are page numbers! (OK, bad Dad joke—I know!)

I know you didn't come here for the jokes, but you get the idea. This isn't going to be your typical snooze-fest tax book. This is where we rip up the rule book and breathe life into taxes, so buckle up, adventurer!

Let's delve into the labyrinth of tax codes, decode the magic of deductions, and unearth the treasure of tax savings. This is your adventure, and it starts now.

Charting Your Course— Understanding the Aggression Scale

Ever wonder how to determine the level of risk you're comfortable with when it comes to taxes? Welcome to the world of the Aggression Scale, a term I coined to measure the risk factor associated with each tax strategy.

This scale runs from 0 to 10, with 0 being as safe as a kitten purring on your lap, and 10 being akin to petting a hungry lion—thrilling, but definitely not advisable.

When you're at 0, it means you're playing it so safe that the IRS will never even glance your way. It's like having a tea party in the middle of a meadow—lovely, but a bit boring. On the other end of the spectrum, at 10, we're all heading to the Big House, and, let me tell you, orange is not the new black in this context.

Every tax strategy has a level of aggression to it, ranging from ultra-conservative 2's to daring 8's. A strategy at 2 suggests that it's so fundamental, your CPA should have known it; if they missed it, it's time to reassess. Strategies at 8 are for those with a taste for adventure and a well-documented paper trail.

Most importantly, you need to determine where you are on this Aggression Scale. Are you more of a 2-3, like most CPAs, favoring caution and peace of mind? Or do you identify as an 8, willing to explore all legal strategies to minimize your tax liability?

Remember, a 9 is the Al Capone zone—doing bad things and hoping not to get caught. No one wants to go there!

At Tax Goddess, we're solid 8's. We're all about aggressive, yet entirely legal, strategies, meticulously documented and above board.

As you navigate this book, keep your personal aggression number in mind as it will help you identify which strategies align with your risk tolerance and financial goals.

However, if you're an audacious 8, ready for some top-notch, big-dollar strategies that go above and beyond what's in this book, don't hesitate to reach out! We have a wealth of knowledge and expertise ready to share with those who are game.

Just remember, tax planning isn't a one-size-fits-all solution; it's about finding the right strategies that fit your unique situation and comfort level.

So, let's embark on this tax adventure and start charting your personalized course.

I highly suggest that you watch this video description as this is an important topic:

TaxGoddess.com/AggressionScale

PART II
STRATEGIES FOR THE 6% LIFE

A Good Tax Plan Is Always Free

> A good tax plan is always free—
> no matter how expensive.
>
> —Dan Henry, founder of
> GetClients.com

THE STRATEGY: CAPTIVE INSURANCE FOR BUSINESS OWNERS

Aggression Scale Level: 4+

Tim rolled out of bed and rubbed the sleep out of his eyes. He grumbled, his mind in that "meh" state. Today was like any other, just another day and another dollar to be earned.

Tim's feet hit the floor, searching for his fuzzy slippers. Finding them, he wiggled his toes in (because damn, that floor was cold without them).

Tim stood up and sleepily stumbled toward the bathroom to brush his teeth and take care of his morning duties. Upon leaving the bathroom, he walked over to his closet and began to pull out the items he would need to get dressed for the day. A pair of socks and undies, a long-sleeved shirt, jeans, and, most importantly, his favorite hoodie—the one with the super warm hood, fleece lined. It was supposed to be a cold one today. However, as Tim glanced out the window to confirm whether it was raining, he noticed that the sky was pretty sunny—a nice unexpected change!

He finished getting dressed and headed downstairs to grab some coffee. His kitchen always made him smile when he walked in.

The best word to describe this gorgeous space was expansive. Granite countertops, a double-wide fridge, and two ovens—specifically for when Pam, Tim's wife, decided to host a dinner party. She makes the most delicious ribs (mouthwatering to even think about it!).

Tim had spent years building his business and working long hours to provide the best he could for his family. All his hard work has finally come to this masterpiece of a kitchen and home for the love of his life, Pam.

About six months ago, Tim was able to buy the dream house that Pam and the kids had always wanted—the gorgeous kitchen, a backyard with a pool, and a huge grass area for their son to practice football with his friends. Tim finally got the woodworking shop he had always wanted. He was no longer relegated to a side corner in the small garage at the old house he used to own.

A smile crossed Tim's face as he saw Pam and the kids happily come into the kitchen after being outside in the garden that morning. Pam had a big basket of fresh vegetables on her hip and looked too adorable in her garden apron.

Tim kissed her on the cheek.

"So, what are you up to today, hun?" Tim asked.

"Nothing much, babe. I'm headed out to have brunch with the girls, so I should be back around 2:30 or 3. You want to do a movie night with the kids tonight?"

Pam is just so awesome—the perfect wife—intelligent, pretty, and a great mom. Tim couldn't have asked for more. That smile would knock over anyone!

"Yeah, that sounds great," Tim said. "I'll order the pizza. Or did you want to make something?"

Pam smiled gently and said, "Pizza would be great if you don't mind. This past week was a little crazy, and even though I love this kitchen, I wouldn't mind a day off from it!"

"Okay, babe. You got it," Tim replied.

As Pam headed out of the kitchen, Tim's smile left his face as his mind drifted to his business.

It had been doing well, but Tim had been putting in 50-60 hours a week to ensure the family had the cash to do what they wanted. The hours were okay, something that he could manage. Still, it was starting to take a toll. He was missing his son's football games, barely making it through the door on time for Pam's dinner parties, coming home late at night, and missing many a movie night.

Pam knew something was wrong; she had even asked him about it several times. But Tim never wanted to make her worry. Instead, he just wanted to be there for his family.

Tim would always tell her that it was okay and that he was "figuring it out." He needed a way to continue making the money the family needed without having to spend all these hours at work.

Tim had been racking his brain for the past year and a half when we first met. But, up until now, no true solutions had presented themselves.

"So let me ask you, Tim. Every business owner wants to keep more of their money and be able to work less but earn more. You're telling me that you've already reached out to your other advisors, and no one has any ideas on how to improve your life on this front?"

On the other end of our Zoom call, Tim appeared to be at his wit's end.

"Yeah, that's right, I've spoken to my financial advisor about what it would take to retire. I am so tired of this. He said that at the current rate that I'm putting money away, it would take at least another 15 years. I know I can do that, but there must be a better way. Missing 15 more years of life isn't worth it," Tim said.

Tim was right. There are always better ways.

Of course, Tim could continue to work for the next 15 years, pay his taxes, and keep what was left to support his family. But, dear reader, if you've picked up this book, you know there's a better way.

Looking at Tim's face, I knew the pain. I had seen it so many times. I had to help him.

Curious, I said, "Tim, let's get this figured out. There are always alternatives. I've analyzed your tax returns and the financial statements for this year's growth, and I have some ideas. Let me ask you, how much money did your advisor say that you needed to put away over the next 15 years to be able to retire?"

Tim, looking defeated, said, "At least another $65,000 a year. So at least $1 million over the next 15 years. I can make that kind of cash, but I will never see my family! I'll be slaving away forever, missing every game and every dinner. I just can't let Pam down. She would be devastated if I had to cut back on time with her and the kids so we can retire in 15 years."

My heart always goes out to entrepreneurs and business owners in this situation. They toil away for years doing their best because they've never had proper tax strategy advice before. They don't know that there are strategies specifically for this situation.

We call these cases "Silent Killers."

As humans, we often only react to things that we can see.

For example, if you have a cut on your leg, you put a Band-Aid on it. Easy to fix, easy to clean, and easy to manage. However, how many of us know beforehand that we're about to have a heart attack or cancer? How many of us feel something wrong internally but don't go to the doctor to check it out because we can't see any outward signs of the issue?

What about pests? How many times do people call out a pest control company because they "saw a bug"? You might have termites crawling around behind your walls. Still, until you see evidence of termites, you don't even bother to get your house protected.

Even worse, bedbugs! How many nasty little things hopped a trip in your luggage from that conference hotel you stayed at while in Vegas? You had no clue until you started seeing bug bites all over your body in your bed at home!

According to Google, there are over 62,000 monthly searches nationwide related to bedbug pest control queries. The second most searched request is termite control!

Between heart diseases, hidden cancers, bedbugs, and termites, there are thousands of Silent Killers around us. Unfortunately, no one focuses on these dangers until they become a significant problem with outward consequences.

Tim was finally seeing the outward consequences of his own Silent Killers. He lacked a strong tax strategy, which led him to overpay his taxes, leaving insufficient cash to fund his retirement sooner (rather than over the next 15 years of living hell).

In a serious tone, I looked at Tim and said, "Tim, I've got options for you, but I need you to understand something. First, you'll have to focus on your Silent Killers and get them under control to set yourself up for true long-term wealth and the free time your family deserves."

Tim's eyes brightened. "I'm ready—let's do this."

One of our most powerful strategies with clients is to utilize an

831(b) program. It's not cheap, but the power of its ROI is spectacular.

An 831(b) is a specific section of the Internal Revenue Code that allows a business to set up an insurance company to manage possible and actual risks to that particular business.

In Tim's case, we found six currently uninsured risks within his business that would allow him to put a little under 15% of his total gross revenue (before expenses) each year into his 831(b) program.

These insurance premiums paid into Tim's 831(b) strategy would be a tax deduction for Tim's primary business (to the tune of approximately $287,500 per year)—earning him a little over $100k/year in tax savings.

Tim was more than able to fund his $65,000/year retirement program. In addition, he had effectively set up his own "bank." A private, secure "bank" offering him easily accessible funds if he ever wanted or needed them. Funds that are 100% tax-free for him and his family.

Now, investing in a tax plan can be expensive, don't get me wrong. In Tim's case, his $75k one-time investment was able to add $100k/year to his take-home in extra tax dollars he got to keep, AND he had $287,500/year added to his private 831(b) bank.

Total savings in Tim's pocket: $387,500 a year!

Tim reduced his 15-year retirement span to less than two and a half years, and the money was easily accessible to Tim for any of his needs. He even ended up spending a little bit upgrading his woodshop—what man can resist new tools?

One of the best parts about a good tax plan is that it can be like a magic sock drawer.

Imagine a sock drawer. It's in a wooden cabinet with some metal handles, and you've opened it and closed it a million times. You've put socks in, you've taken socks out, and you've even lost a few socks to the sock gnomes (you know, the ones that always steal your left-foot sock).

What you didn't know is that some sock drawers are magic.

Magic sock drawers double the amount of cash put into them.

So, when someone puts cash in this sock drawer, the cash doubles.

Every time someone puts cash in the drawer, the cash doubles.

A good tax strategy plan is just like a magic sock drawer. It may take some money investment (you've got to put some money into the drawer), but the cash that comes out of the drawer often has massive ROI. I note that for most tax strategies, a 2X ROI is acceptable, but we always strive for more value. For example, the current average ROI on the 831(b) tax strategy alone is over 7X when done correctly.

❝
Price is what you pay.
Value is what you get.

—Warren Buffett

The Implementation

Setting up a captive insurance company under Code Section 831(b) can be a complex process, requiring careful planning, compliance with numerous regulations, and ongoing maintenance. Here is a step-by-step guidebook to create and set up a captive insurance company:

Step 1: Assess your business needs.

Evaluate the risks your business faces and determine whether a captive insurance company could be an effective risk management tool for your organization.

Step 2: Assemble a team of professionals.

Hire a team of experienced professionals, including a captive manager, attorneys, accountants, actuaries, and investment managers, to help you navigate the process and ensure compliance with all regulatory requirements.

Step 3: Choose a domicile.

Research various domiciles for your captive insurance company, considering factors such as regulatory environment, taxation, infrastructure, and access to professional services. Your domicile can be either a U.S. state or an offshore jurisdiction.

Step 4: Develop a business plan.

Work with your team to create a comprehensive business plan, outlining your captive's operations, management structure, underwriting, and investment strategies.

Step 5: Apply for a license.

Submit a license application to the regulatory authority in your chosen domicile. This will typically include your business plan, financial projections, and other relevant documentation.

Step 6: Capitalize the captive.

Fund your captive insurance company with the required capital, in accordance with the regulatory requirements of your chosen domicile.

Step 7: Set up the operational infrastructure.

Establish the operational infrastructure for your captive, including IT systems, office space, and staffing, as needed.

Step 8: Issue policies.

Begin underwriting insurance policies for your parent company and/or affiliated companies.

Step 9: Manage the captive.

Oversee the ongoing operations, investments, and risk management of your captive insurance company, ensuring compliance with all regulatory and reporting requirements.

Step 10: Annual compliance and reporting

Each year, both the captive insurance company and its owner must file various forms with their tax returns, including:

- Form 1120-PC: The captive must file this form to report its income, gains, losses, deductions, credits, and to calculate its tax liability.

- Form 8886: The captive and its owner should file this form if the captive is considered a reportable transaction under IRS guidelines.

- Form 8918: The captive must file this form if it is considered a material advisor to a reportable transaction.

- Form 5471: If the captive is a controlled foreign corporation (CFC), the U.S. owner must file this form to report information about the CFC.

- Form 8938: U.S. owners of specified foreign financial assets, including interests in a CFC, may be required to file this form to report those assets.

- Form 8621: If the captive is a passive foreign investment company (PFIC), U.S. shareholders may need to file this form to report income and gains from the PFIC.

Remember that setting up and maintaining a captive insurance company under Section 831(b) is a complex process that requires the guidance of experienced professionals. This guidebook is not exhaustive and should be considered as a starting point for understanding the steps involved in creating a captive insurance company.

The Pitfalls

Owning and operating a captive insurance company comes with its own set of challenges and potential pitfalls. Here are some of the most common issues that businesses may face:

- Insufficient capitalization: Inadequate capitalization can lead to financial instability and an inability to meet claims obligations which can jeopardize the captive's viability and result in regulatory scrutiny.

- Inadequate risk distribution: Captive insurance companies need to have proper risk distribution to maintain their tax-advantaged status. Failing to achieve this can result in unfavorable tax consequences and potential penalties.

- Noncompliance with regulatory requirements: Failing to comply with the regulations of the chosen domicile or other applicable jurisdictions can lead to fines, penalties, or even the revocation of the captive's license.

- Overreliance on third-party service providers: While it is common to engage third-party service providers for various aspects of captive operations, overreliance on them can lead to a lack of internal control and oversight, potentially exposing the captive to additional risks.

- Ineffective risk management: Failing to implement robust risk management practices can result in increased exposure to risks and potential losses, undermining the purpose of the captive insurance company.

- Lack of corporate governance: Poor corporate governance, including inadequate oversight by the board of directors and a lack of clear policies and procedures, can lead to operational inefficiencies and an increased risk of noncompliance with regulatory requirements.

- Inadequate underwriting and pricing: Inaccurate underwriting and pricing of risks can lead to financial losses as the captive may not collect sufficient premiums to cover its claims obligations.

- Misuse of captive for tax evasion: The IRS closely scrutinizes captive insurance companies to ensure they are not being used for tax evasion purposes. Engaging in aggressive tax planning or using the captive primarily for tax benefits can result in significant penalties and potential legal consequences.

- Inefficient claims handling: Inadequate or inefficient claims handling processes can lead to delayed payments, increased costs, and dissatisfaction among the insured parties.

- Lack of diversification: Focusing on a single line of business or industry can expose the captive to concentration risk, which could result in significant losses if the insured risks materialize.

To mitigate these potential pitfalls, it is crucial to work closely with experienced professionals, including attorneys, tax advisors, and captive insurance consultants, and to maintain strong internal controls, corporate governance, and risk management practices.

Extreme Cases That Will Get You Thrown in Jail (Or Cause Otherwise Severe Penalties, Issues, or Problems for You!)

I want to seriously reiterate this point: **Misuse of captive for tax evasion**. The IRS closely scrutinizes captive insurance companies to ensure they are not being used for tax evasion purposes. Engaging in aggressive tax planning or using the captive primarily for tax benefits can result in significant penalties and potential legal consequences.

The IRS Dirty Dozen List is an annual compilation of tax scams and schemes that taxpayers should be aware of and avoid. This list highlights the most prevalent and aggressive tactics used by unscrupulous individuals and entities to commit tax fraud or evade taxes.

In recent years, the IRS has included both captive insurance companies and conservation easements on this list, indicating that these legitimate tax planning strategies have been increasingly abused for tax evasion purposes.

Captive insurance companies can offer significant tax benefits when properly structured and operated for genuine risk management purposes. However, some taxpayers have misused captives to generate excessive premium deductions, funnel income to related parties, or engage in other abusive practices.

The IRS has stepped up its scrutiny of captive insurance companies, particularly those structured under Code Section 831(b), which allows for special tax treatment of small insurance companies.

To ensure that your captive insurance company does not come under scrutiny by the IRS, it is essential to follow certain best practices. First and foremost, make sure your captive is formed and operated for legitimate risk management purposes and not solely for tax benefits. Establish proper risk distribution, either by insuring a diverse pool of risks or by participating in a risk-sharing arrangement with other captives or commercial insurers.

Maintain accurate and detailed documentation of your captive's operations, including underwriting guidelines, risk assessments, and claims handling processes. This documentation will be crucial if your captive is ever audited by the IRS.

Additionally, work closely with experienced professionals, such as attorneys, tax advisors, and captive insurance consultants, to ensure that your captive complies with all relevant regulations and best practices.

If You Want to Know More (Bonus)

We receive hundreds of messages asking for more details about the inner workings of the 831(b) and how you can effectively access your funds while also enjoying a tax deduction.

As a tax strategist, my mission in this book is to equip you with the essential knowledge on tax strategies that have the potential to greatly impact your life.

I am committed to providing you with comprehensive insights into the strategies discussed here.

In *The 6% Life*, I have crafted the tax strategies to be timeless, as the opportunity they present has remained relatively stable since the 1986 tax reform.

However, it is important to note that the IRS conducts an annual review of this strategy due to its significant power, aiming to prevent any misuse. Unfortunately, some unscrupulous individuals have exploited this strategy for nefarious purposes, which has resulted in its inclusion on the IRS Dirty Dozen List for multiple consecutive years.

To safeguard yourself, it is crucial to work with reputable providers when employing this strategy. If you don't know how to set up an 831(b) program, you don't feel comfortable doing this, or your CPA tells you no (or worse, seems unaware of this strategy in the first place), then please access our page dedicated to this strategy at **TaxGoddess.com/831b.** In this bonus, I cover in a detailed video how the program works and the benefits to you and your business.

Since this strategy should be implemented within a comprehensive plan, the provided details are generally applicable and may not cover all circumstances. Additionally, if you have any inquiries regarding the bonus PDF download, feel free to schedule a chat with my team.

Kids—Just Cute? No, a Supreme Tax Advantage

❝

The single biggest problem in communication is the illusion that it has taken place.

—George Bernard Shaw

The Strategy: Paying Your Children 100% Tax-Free

Aggression Scale Level: 2+

Steve owns two landscaping businesses. He works long days, often 10 to 12 hours on the road watching his crews—ensuring the jobs go smoothly to provide support for his growing family.

Amanda, Steve's wife, manages not only the household (seven children ranging in age from 4 to 11—a big brood by anyone's standard) but also all the finances for the business. Every time I meet her she has a smile on her face and is positive and upbeat.

I remember the first time they came to my office. It was a sunshine-filled day here in Arizona. Steve and Amanda pulled up in a large grey F350 and parked outside my office window. I could see them unloading kids from the car and heading around to our front entrance. Amanda was already far along in her pregnancy with child number eight and was doing a little bit of the pregnant mother waddle as she walked across the parking lot.

When they had originally filled out my mini-questionnaire so that I knew who I was meeting with, I was absolutely expecting Steve to handle this conversation. However, as soon as we sat down, Amanda handed Steve the two children and told him to keep the kids busy. She pulled out some crayons, and Steve and the kids went to sit on my couch in the far corner of my office to help the kids color.

Once everyone was settled, Amanda turned to me and said, "We are so excited to meet with someone like you. Our current CPAs just aren't providing any strategy, so we've been interviewing for a new team. We've met with quite a few other CPA firms, but none of them talk about tax strategy at all, and certainly not the way you do—you've got such passion about it! Everyone else has been the same old, same old stuffy CPA firm!"

I laughed a little with a bit of an impish smile. "Aww! That's sweet! Well, I do love what I do," I said.

As a Certified Tax Specialist and Certified Tax Coach, I've heard this over and over and over again: my current CPA does not provide any tax strategies (even when asked specifically about strategies). Not surprising really, since there are only 607 specialists in the entire U.S. certified to do the type of work we do.

Amanda continued, "I've been through your YouTube channel and watched at least 20 of your videos. I love how your mind thinks. I can't wait to get into our meeting today. I know you have tax strategies, and I think that there are a few good ones that might apply to us.

"As you can tell by the information that we filled out online, we have two businesses, both of which are doing pretty well.

Steve is working so hard, and even though he is doing an amazing job, he keeps hoping that working harder will bring in the money that we need to meet our goals. I'm worried about being able to really keep more money for our family. The harder he works, the more taxes we pay, and less and less is coming into the family home. We have a large family, which Steve and I really enjoy. We want to get to at least 10 children, if not more. My primary goal is to keep as much money as possible for our family, as well as set ourselves up for retirement and continue to grow the crews for our business so that the business income can support more and more of our family needs."

I smiled to myself, thinking, *I like this lady already! Direct, to the point, and in control of her situation.*

Amanda said, "One of the videos on your YouTube channel talked about paying your children. Considering we have so many, I've been waiting to ask you this question. How would a strategy like this be implementable for our business?"

Now, dear reader, let me ask you something. What would you do in this situation …

You went to bed last night feeling slightly under the weather. You tossed and turned all night, throwing off the blankets, then shivering, then covering back up because you were freezing to death.

When you wake up the next morning, your eyes are red from lack of sleep, your back hurts, your throat is completely sore, and you can barely speak. Your nose is running, and your head feels like somebody inflated a big red balloon inside of it.

What is your next step?

You might go to your bathroom cabinet and pull out some cold medicine, maybe take a couple of Nyquil, and call your boss to take the day off from work.

You hope that taking a day off and getting some really good sleep, knocked out by some strong drugs, might help you clear up what is clearly the common cold.

But what if that doesn't cut it?

Two weeks later, you are now completely exhausted, can barely get out of bed, certainly can't drive anywhere, and literally look like a zombie every time you leave your bedroom (sunken eyes, craving for food but can't eat it as the thought of food makes you sick to your stomach).

You've done absolutely everything that you can think of—a visit to your family doctor to get some serious high-power drugs, Grandma's chicken soup, ancient homeopathic acupuncture, and even taken it as far as calling down to New Orleans to see to find a voodoo magician to see if they could do anything.

After two weeks off from work, your boss is starting to think that you have quit your job, and you're in danger of being unable to pay your upcoming mortgage.

What are you going to do now?

When you've got a specialty problem, you need a specialist to handle it.

And if you continue to take a specialist problem to a generalist, you're going to end up paying for it one way or another.

As entrepreneurs, you have specialist problems, not generalist standard CPA problems.

You've literally become the walking dead. It's time for something more drastic—something is definitely wrong.

You call your GP and demand that he helps you find a specialist. You book an appointment at the Mayo Clinic.

You admit that it's a little bit scary that your GP doesn't seem to have any clue what's going on and your mind begins to race. Is this some sort of cancer? Is this some sort of West Nile virus that you caught from that trip you went on? Is this something that you will recover from or are you slowly going to fade away into black?

At least the good part is the Mayo Clinic has a cancellation for an appointment only three days from now, so you only have to hold on and suffer until then.

After multiple tests, scans, exams, and pokes/prods, one of the top cancer specialists comes into your room with a very serious look on his face.

"You've got cancer. It's a very aggressive form, however, you came in soon enough. I believe I'll be able to remove it all with surgery. That surgery is scheduled for tomorrow morning. How do you want to proceed?"

> Hope is not a strategy.
>
> —Fred Kroin

Hoping that the drugs, acupuncture, and voodoo magic were going to save you was not enough.

Hope is not a strategy.

You implemented a strategy. You demanded a specialist.

And thank goodness you did. Your life was saved because you DID something about your situation rather than hoping it would get better.

Steve and Amanda stopped hoping that their CPA was going to DO something for them. They implemented a strategy. For Steve and Amanda, that strategy was as clear as day to me.

"We need to get those kids on payroll. That's going to save you a significant amount of money every year," I said.

The IRS allows any child over the age of seven to work in a family business, and the business is allowed to take a tax deduction of the amount paid to the child.

The work can be paid for at reasonable compensation (which can match the amount you pay an adult for the same job) and any amount up to about $19,850/year is 100% tax-free to the kids and a 100% tax deduction for the parent's business.

You pay the child via a W-2, which allows you to put away into a child's retirement to start building their assets while they are young. The child can use this money either to invest and grow savings or pay for anything that is not a parental duty (so no food, clothing, or shelter expenses).

Best yet, if you are paying from a Schedule C sole proprietorship, all of this money is 100% tax-free to both the parents and the child—no federal tax, state tax, FICA tax, or Medicare tax. **It's literally 100% tax-free.**

Considering the fact that Steve and Amanda currently have five children between the ages of 7 and 17, they now had an instantaneous tax deduction of over $99,250 per year.

At their current tax bracket of 32%, this was going to put an extra $31,760/year back into their pockets without any trouble from the IRS or significant complex strategy on their part.

The family just made $99,250 per year completely tax-free.

Amanda was stunned. She sat in silence for a minute and leaned back in the chair. She looked over at Steve, who smiled, and then looked back at me and said, "You know, honestly, after seeing your YouTube video on the subject, I've asked every CPA that we've met with about the strategy, and not one of them could explain it as easily as you just did to me. Those other CPAs were using so much technical language that I couldn't even understand or relate to what they were saying.

"This strategy makes complete and utter sense for our family. It's perfect for us! I am so happy we came in today," she said, grinning from ear to ear. "I can't believe that you literally just saved us $99,000 in our first meeting! I can't wait to see what you do for us in the upcoming years as your new clients."

Steve and Amanda became new clients of ours that day. To date, and with her current brood of children (now at 10 kids),

KIDS—JUST CUTE? NO, A SUPREME TAX ADVANTAGE

Steve and Amanda have made their family over $1.3 million in tax-free income using this single strategy alone.

If Amanda had not continued to ask questions, reaching out for communication and knowledge, she and Steve would still be in the same place they were before they met us—significantly overpaying the government and handing over all of their hard-earned cash.

By questioning the status quo provided by their previous CPAs, asking questions, communicating, finding a specialist, and following the instructions of the specialist, Steve and Amanda are now two very happy campers.

Remember, not all CPAs are tax strategists! According to Google, there are over 660,000 CPAs in the entire U.S., but the AICTC only recognizes 15 Certified Tax Strategists. We are one of them.

If you want significant results, you need to use a specialist. Don't let your tax tumor be overlooked by your GP CPA.

> Research is creating new knowledge.
>
> –Neil Armstrong

The Implementation

Paying your children through your business can be an effective tax and financial planning strategy. Here's an implementation guide on how to pay your kids through your business and contribute to their Traditional or Roth IRA using their earned income for a double bonus on your money:

Step 1: Evaluate the suitability.

Determine whether employing your children in your business is appropriate and feasible. Consider their ages, abilities, and the type of work they can perform.

Step 2: Define the job responsibilities.

Create a clear job description for each child, outlining their roles and responsibilities within your business.

Step 3: Establish a reasonable compensation.

Determine a fair and reasonable compensation for the work your children will perform. Ensure that the compensation is comparable to what you would pay an unrelated employee for similar work.

Step 4: Ensure compliance with labor laws.

Familiarize yourself with federal and state labor laws, particularly those related to employing minors, and ensure your business is in compliance with all applicable regulations.

Step 5: Prepare employment documents.

Prepare the necessary employment documents, such as an employment agreement, Form W-4 (Employee's Withholding Allowance Certificate), and Form I-9 (Employment Eligibility Verification). Keep these documents on file, just as you would for any other employee.

Step 6: Pay your children through your business.

Process your children's payroll, either by issuing paychecks or through direct deposit. Ensure that all applicable payroll taxes are withheld and remitted to the appropriate tax authorities.

Step 7: Keep accurate records.

Maintain accurate records of the work your children perform, the hours they work, and the wages they earn. This documentation will be important for tax purposes and in the event of an audit.

Step 8: Report the income on your child's tax return.

Your children will need to file their own tax returns to report their earned income. If they are required to file a return, ensure that they do so timely and accurately.

Step 9: Open a Traditional or Roth IRA for your child.

Open an IRA account in your child's name, either a Traditional or Roth IRA, depending on your child's age, income, and financial goals. Consult with a financial advisor to determine which type of IRA is best for your child's situation.

Step 10: Contribute to the IRA using your child's earned income.

Make contributions to your child's IRA using their earned income, up to the annual contribution limit or the amount of their earned income, whichever is less. For 2023, the annual contribution limit is $6,000.

By following these steps, you can effectively employ your children in your business and help them save for their future by contributing to their Traditional or Roth IRA using their earned income. Remember to consult with a tax professional and financial advisor to ensure compliance with all applicable laws and regulations.

The Pitfalls

When attempting to pay their children through their business, people may encounter various pitfalls or problems that can arise from doing it incorrectly. Some of these issues include:

- Noncompliance with labor laws: Failing to comply with federal and state labor laws, particularly those related to employing minors, can result in fines, penalties, and potential legal issues.

- Unreasonable compensation: Paying children an excessive salary that isn't in line with the fair market value for the work performed can raise red flags with the IRS and may lead to disallowed deductions.

- Inadequate documentation: Not maintaining proper records of the work performed, hours worked, and wages paid can create issues during an IRS audit and may result in disallowed deductions or penalties.

- Failure to withhold and remit payroll taxes: Not properly withholding and remitting payroll taxes for your children can result in tax penalties and interest.

- Not issuing proper tax forms: Failing to issue the appropriate tax forms, such as Form W-2, can lead to penalties and make it difficult for your children to accurately report their income on their tax returns.

- Mixing personal and business expenses: Paying children for personal tasks or services unrelated to the business can jeopardize the legitimacy of the arrangement and may result in disallowed deductions.

- Not reporting income on your child's tax return: Neglecting to report your child's earned income on their tax return can result in penalties, interest, and potential tax issues.

- Exceeding IRA contribution limits: Contributing more than the annual limit or your child's earned income to their IRA can result in excess contribution penalties.

To avoid these pitfalls and problems, ensure that you follow all applicable laws and regulations, maintain proper documentation, and consult with a tax professional and financial advisor when implementing this strategy.

Extreme Cases That Will Get You Thrown in Jail (Or Cause Otherwise Severe Penalties, Issues, or Problems for You!)

While there may not be a specific high-profile IRS court case related to paying children incorrectly, there have been instances where taxpayers faced issues due to improperly employing and compensating their children. In some cases, the IRS has disallowed deductions for wages paid to children or questioned the legitimacy of the arrangement.

For example, in the case of Eller v. Commissioner (T.C. Memo. 1988-250), the court disallowed a business owner's deductions for wages paid to their children because they failed to substantiate the payment of wages or show that the wages were reasonable for the work performed. In this case, the taxpayer did not provide sufficient documentation to prove that the children were bona fide employees and that the wages paid were consistent with the fair market value for the services rendered.

In Eller v. Commissioner, the court disallowed the business owner's deductions for wages paid to their children, finding that the taxpayer failed to substantiate the payment of wages or demonstrate that the wages were reasonable for the work performed. As a result, the deductions claimed for the wages paid to the children were disallowed, leading to an increase in the taxpayer's taxable income and a higher tax liability.

In addition to the disallowed deductions, the taxpayer in Eller v. Commissioner was also subject to potential penalties and interest associated with the underpayment of taxes. These penalties and interest charges can vary depending on the specific circumstances of the case, but they can be substantial, especially if the underpayment of taxes is deemed to be due to negligence or disregard for the rules and regulations.

This example illustrates the importance of maintaining proper documentation, ensuring compliance with all applicable laws and regulations, and consulting with a tax professional when implementing a strategy to pay your children through your business. By doing so, you can minimize the risk of facing issues with the IRS and maximize the potential benefits of this strategy.

If You Want to Know More (BONUS)

Many of you want to know more about the specific details on how to pay your children properly to keep the IRS happy and get these amazing benefits.

My job as a tax strategist, especially in this book, is to give you the details on tax strategies that could significantly change your life, so I want to ensure you get the details on any strategies I speak about here.

Please note that I've written *The 6% Life* so that the tax strategies are, to the best of my ability, evergreen. Since the opportunity to pay your kids has been around since 1986, I don't think this strategy will change drastically anytime soon.

However, because the rules around this strategy change yearly, I am careful not to include specific numbers in this book as to the dollar limits, contribution amounts, rules, etc.

If you'd like more details on this particular strategy, please go to our website and download the bonus for this chapter—a free, up-to-date PDF on the steps and items you need to know specifically about this strategy.

The website for this strategy:

TaxGoddess.com/PayMyKids

KIDS—JUST CUTE? NO, A SUPREME TAX ADVANTAGE

You can also book a time to chat with my team if you have any questions on this PDF, and you are welcome to take it to your CPA to have them look over the details.

Since the strategy should be implemented as a part of an overall plan, the details are general in nature and may not apply in all circumstances.

Massively Fund Your Retirement, Even if You Are Way Behind the Eight Ball— Two Heads Are Better than One

❝

The single biggest problem in communication is the illusion that it has taken place.

—George Bernard Shaw

The Strategy: Defined Benefit, Cash Balance, and 401(k) Programs

Aggression Scale Level: -2
(Every CPA should know this one!)

"My partner is used to the accountant we have, so it's hard to change," said Max. Max had been following up with our team for years. Calling in, asking for help and strategies that he could apply to his taxes. Anything. He knew that he needed some sort of change. He had paid, on average, over $130,000 a year in taxes to the government for the past seven years. And every year or two, we've had the same discussion …

I replied, "Max, you know I'm here to help. But, we've had so many discussions about this. So, maybe it's time for me to talk to your partner, RJ, about this. Your tax situation will never change if he doesn't understand that we work **with** your CPA, not against him. We are another pair of eyes—trained to find the strategies even really good CPAs miss."

"I know, I know. Yeah, let me see what I can do here. Enough is enough, and I am getting tired of it," Max sighed as we got off the phone.

RJ was Max's long-time business partner. From what I was told, RJ prided himself on being the more knowledgeable of the two, always doing the research and finding opportunities.

I questioned this when I brought up the idea of using a defined benefit program to massively pump up their retirement accounts. Max had never heard of it!

"Wait," Max said. "So you're telling me that because we're both in our mid-50s, each of us can put away a little over $170,000 a year into our retirement accounts?! And it is completely tax-deductible?! RJ told me that based on his research and our CPA, the maximum we could do is $60,000 a year into our 401(k)."

"Well, I can't say that surprises me," I said. "Many CPAs know the basics and do their best with their strategies and training, but they don't necessarily know some of the more advanced tactics. This is why we work so well as a team with your CPA—it is our job to know these advanced strategies, and your CPA can implement them into your taxes, so you save a ton of money each year."

"I've got to bring this up to RJ," Max said, seemingly now determined to get this new strategy to work for him.

A few weeks passed, and I saw that Max had booked a time on my calendar for us to chat with RJ in tow.

We reached the meeting day, and I could tell by RJ's body language that he really didn't want to be there. He had his arms crossed, sitting back from the table with his body slightly turned away from me. He was professional; he knew I was a CPA, but obviously, he wasn't very interested in hearing what I had to say. Clearly, he was only in this meeting at Max's request.

On the other hand, Max was beaming—grinning ear to ear. This was the first time RJ had agreed to at least sit down and chat with me about strategy.

"I am so excited for you to tell RJ and me more about this defined benefit strategy you brought up a few weeks ago, Shauna. I really want RJ to be able to ask questions and get into the details on how this could help us," Max said.

"OK," I said, "Let's get down to brass tacks then and see what we can do." I smiled (knowing exactly what we could do).

I went into consulting mode—working to solve the problem—focused on the best outcome for Max and RJ together.

Looking at RJ, I said, "RJ, Max tells me that you are the detailed researcher between the two of you. In some of the more recent conversations I've had with Max, he's been really bothered. He has talked about how he wants to reduce his taxes and how his retirement accounts balance, or lack thereof, is bugging him. He worries that it isn't going to be enough since he is already 56 this year. How are you feeling about your tax burden and your retirement right now?"

"Well," RJ said, scoffing, "I'm fine with it. It is what it is. I know that I am paying the minimum taxes that we can because my CPA, John, tells us that there's nothing more that can be done for our accounts. He's got 30+ years of experience, so I believe him. Whenever I ask him if there are any new strategies, he says there is nothing else we can do to reduce our taxes. John has never gotten us in trouble or had any problems, so I don't want to get into some scheme that will put a red flag on my account with the IRS or something like that! My retirement is good enough. It would be great if the government would change the rules to allow me to put in more, but it is what it is."

I understood. I've had similar conversations with thousands of clients before Max and RJ.

I looked at the paperwork in front of me. It was an Excel spreadsheet with all the detailed backup source information for a defined benefit program. In addition, it listed the figures on how much money I would save RJ and Max by implementing this program. I slid the spreadsheet across my desk to RJ, feeling the texture of the paper under my fingers and the slight breeze from the air conditioning fluttering the corner of the page.

"What's this?" RJ asked.

"This is how you're going to increase your retirement and save a ton of money. You could increase your contributions from $60,000/year to $170,000/year each—saving you each an additional $49,500/year in cold hard cash on your taxes every single year. This is a strategy called a defined benefit program."

Now, my dear reader, did you know that not all CPAs know about defined benefit programs?

Defined benefit programs have been around since the 1800s. They are more secure and stable than other types of plans. Huge companies like American Express, Johnson & Johnson, and the U.S. Armed Forces have utilized them for hundreds of years.

It wasn't until 1978 that the government introduced 401(k) programs via The Revenue Act of 1978. The U.S. government massively promoted these 401(k) programs to the public and corporations, saying: "Oh, here is this awesome new thing; everyone should use it." So, everyone switched over to it. Over time, most CPAs and employers forgot about the defined benefit plan. Instead, they focused on the 401(k), which is how it became mainstream. Because 401(k)s became so popularized, most CPAs and accountants just default to using a 401(k) plan. In reality, the defined benefit plan could save you more money—a viable and legal loophole on the IRS books.

Let's use a mini case here.

Did you know that it's a law that you cannot use a false name at a hotel in New Hampshire? Strange, but OK. If somebody wanted to sue you because you used a false name at a hotel in New Hampshire, they would win in a court of law because the old rule is still on the books!

Old rules can help get you what you want, just as in the case of RJ and Max. The old law of defined benefit programs will allow RJ and Max to massively increase their retirement contributions and reduce their tax burdens currently.

RJ made an incredulous face and said, "Wait, what? $170k? There is no way; how did my CPA not know about this?!"

"Well, let's chat through that. Do you know who Warren Buffett is?" I asked.

"Of course, who doesn't know who Warren Buffett is?" RJ asked, a little taken aback at the question.

"Fair," I laughed. "OK, then you know who Charlie Munger is, right?"

"Well, yes, he's Warren Buffett's partner … What does Charlie Munger have to do with this?" RJ said.

So, I began to tell the story …

"Warren Buffett says that he would not be as successful as he is today without Charlie's 'No Cigar-Butt' investing model—looking for long-term investments, companies that would be successful for a long period of time rather than those that might have only 'one puff left in the cigar.' Likewise, Charlie has said that he would not be the success he is today without Warren's 'Oracle of Omaha' investing genius, his big picture ideas, and strategic thinking."

RJ's face showed he was listening. It was the first time I had seen that he was opening up a bit.

I kept speaking.

"Having a CPA and a Tax Strategist is like the relationship between Warren and Charlie. Both need each other. They sometimes disagree, but they respect each other's knowledge and skills. Open-mindedness is why the relationship is so successful and why it is so lucrative for their investors. Neither of them let their egos get in the way of making great business decisions. Because they work together, they are a powerhouse investing team. Having two heads working on a problem is better than one."

RJ pondered this as I said, "So, you can imagine, if John and I work together on your behalf, like Warren and Charlie, how many other strategies can we find for you?"

RJ sat back in his chair, the piece of paper in hand, while he looked at the numbers I had presented.

"So you see," I said, "The client always wins when there are two pairs of eyes. Two heads are always better than one, especially when those two heads, your CPA and your Tax Strategist, have multiple solutions that they can provide. My job as a Tax Strategist is to bring new solutions that your CPA doesn't know. Solutions above the basics are generally strategies that most CPAs don't have the time, bandwidth, or desire to research. They are usually too busy preparing tax returns and keeping the IRS off your back."

"Huh," said RJ, showing his interest. "So you're telling me this strategy is 100% approved by the IRS? This isn't going to get us in trouble, right?"

I smiled. My company, Tax Goddess, had already set up thousands of these plans. None of them had been audited. None of them had ever had any troubles. And all of them have produced fantastic tax write-offs for our clients.

"That's what I'm telling you, RJ. This is a completely legal, above-board, tried and tested strategy. It's a perfect way for both of you to get tax deductions and fund significantly more into your retirement accounts.

"I would happily sit with your CPA, John, and review every detail. He can ask me any questions. We can even review the examples and court cases to ensure that your CPA feels as comfortable with this strategy as I do. We work with him to produce the best results for you. So you can keep your 30-year CPA relationship with John AND get all of the tax write-offs you are legally allowed to by us all working together."

Max, who had been sitting this whole time silently watching his partner's reactions, jumped forward to the edge of his seat.

"See!" Max said. "What did I tell you? We've got to at least have the meeting with John and Shauna and see if John agrees to this. If it can save us almost $100,000 a year, why would we not do this?!"

RJ nodded in reflective thought.

After a few minutes, RJ raised his head from the calculations paper and said, "OK, let's chat with John."

Max did it! (With help from a Tax Goddess and the IRS code.) That next week RJ, Max, and I met with John.

Though I have done sessions like these thousands of times, I am always a little nervous going into CPA meetings. What if the CPA isn't open-minded? What if the CPA feels threatened by my presence? What if the CPA says no only because they don't want to learn new things?

I prepared myself, as always, with the most details possible and was armed and ready to walk into that meeting with John.

What I thought was going to be a very tough meeting turned out to be a pleasant, collaborative, and fruitful discussion. John was thrilled to have a professional Tax Strategist who specialized in finding above-board, legal tax loopholes on the team.

After our meeting, John called me. He said, in a cheerful tone, "I know that Max and RJ have been asking for more strategies, and honestly, being an expert in tax strategy has never been my thing. So I wasn't sure what to say as I didn't want to look bad to my clients. But I'm happy that Max found you and brought you in."

By the end of our meeting, John, RJ, Max, and I had agreed to a basic outline of tax strategies. We even found a few more in our joint meeting, including some overdue entity structuring. Total savings? Max would save over $73,000/year in taxes and RJ over $84,000/year.

RJ was smiling. Finally.

And Max? Today, he looked giddy—like a five-year-old with a new lollipop. (For $73k, he could buy quite a few lollipops!)

A good CPA or tax preparer always wants an excellent team to help their clients. They want to work with an expert, a second pair of eyes. They want to work with a specialist—someone who can really save their clients thousands of dollars. A good CPA will always bring in a Tax Strategist to work on your client team because they know that if they save you thousands of dollars by bringing in experts, you will be their CPA client for life.

The Implementation

Forming a defined benefit program, cash balance program, and offering 401(k) options for your business involves several steps and requires careful planning, compliance with various regulations, and ongoing maintenance. Here's an implementation guide to help you set up these programs:

Step 1: Evaluate the feasibility.

Assess the feasibility of offering these retirement plans based on your business size, financial resources, and employee needs.

Step 2: Assemble a team of professionals.

Hire a team of experienced professionals, including retirement plan consultants, attorneys, accountants, and investment advisors, to help you navigate the process and ensure compliance with all regulatory requirements.

Step 3: Design the plan.

Work with your team to design the defined benefit program, cash balance program, and 401(k) plan, taking into consideration factors such as eligibility, vesting, contribution formulas, and benefit payment options.

Step 4: Prepare plan documents.

Draft the necessary plan documents, including a written plan document, summary plan description, and any required notices. Ensure that the plan documents comply with the Employee Retirement Income Security Act (ERISA) and other applicable regulations.

Step 5: Establish a trust fund.

Set up a trust fund to hold and manage the plan assets. Appoint a trustee to oversee the trust and ensure that the assets are used solely for the benefit of the plan participants and their beneficiaries.

Step 6: Choose plan investments.

Select the investment options for your 401(k) plan, ensuring that they meet the diversification requirements and provide participants with an adequate range of investment choices.

Step 7: Set up recordkeeping and administration.

Establish a system for maintaining plan records and administering the plan, either in-house or by outsourcing to a third-party administrator. This includes tracking participant accounts, processing contributions, and calculating benefits.

Step 8: Enroll employees.

Provide eligible employees with information about the plan, including a summary plan description and any required notices. Ensure that employees have the opportunity to enroll in the 401(k) plan and make contribution elections.

Step 9: Manage the plan.

Oversee the ongoing operations and investments of the plan,

ensuring compliance with all regulatory and reporting requirements. Monitor the plan's performance, review plan fees, and make any necessary adjustments to the plan design or investments.

Step 10: Annual compliance and reporting

Ensure that your business complies with annual reporting, testing, and disclosure requirements, including:

- Form 5500: File this form annually to report financial and other plan-related information to the Department of Labor and IRS.

- Nondiscrimination testing: Perform required testing to ensure that the plan does not disproportionately benefit highly compensated employees.

- Participant statements: Provide annual statements to plan participants, detailing their account balances, vesting status, and investment performance.

- Summary Annual Report (SAR): Distribute the SAR to plan participants, summarizing the financial information reported on Form 5500.

Step 11: Process payroll and tax filings.

From a payroll and tax filing perspective, ensure that you:

- Withhold employee 401(k) contributions from their paychecks and remit them to the plan's trust fund.

- Process employer contributions, such as matching or profit-sharing contributions, as specified in the plan documents.

- Report plan contributions and other relevant information on employees' Form W-2.

- Deduct employer contributions on your business tax return, subject to applicable limits and regulations.

This guide is not exhaustive and should be considered a starting point for understanding the steps involved in creating a defined benefit program, cash balance program, and offering 401(k) options. Consult with experienced professionals to ensure that you comply with all applicable laws and regulations.

The Pitfalls

Creating and maintaining a defined benefit program, cash balance program, and offering 401(k) options can be complex, and there are several pitfalls and problems that may arise. Here are some common areas where people might make mistakes or encounter issues:

- Noncompliance with regulations: Failing to comply with ERISA, IRS, and Department of Labor (DOL) regulations can lead to penalties, fines, and even disqualification of the plan.

- Inadequate plan design: Poorly designed plans may not meet the needs of employees, fail to attract and retain talent, or be unnecessarily expensive to maintain.

- Inaccurate calculations: Errors in calculating contributions or benefits can result in overpayments, underpayments, or noncompliance with regulatory requirements.

- Failure to conduct nondiscrimination testing: Not performing the required nondiscrimination tests or failing to correct any identified issues can result in penalties and jeopardize the plan's tax-qualified status.

- Lack of proper documentation: Not maintaining accurate and up-to-date plan documents, records, and disclosures can lead to compliance issues and make it difficult to manage the plan effectively.

- Insufficient monitoring of investments: Failing to regularly review and monitor plan investments can result in poor investment performance, excessive fees, or noncompliance with fiduciary responsibilities.

- Inadequate communication with employees: Not providing employees with timely and accurate information about the plan can lead to confusion, low participation rates, and potential legal issues.

- Late or incorrect reporting: Failing to file required forms, such as Form 5500, or submitting them late or with errors can result in penalties and potential compliance issues.

- Not addressing changes in the business or regulatory environment: Failing to adjust the plan in response to changes in your business or evolving regulations can lead to noncompliance, financial risks, or suboptimal plan performance.

- Insufficient fiduciary oversight: Not properly fulfilling fiduciary responsibilities, such as selecting and monitoring service providers, can result in legal liabilities and potential financial losses for the plan and its participants.

To avoid these pitfalls and problems, work with experienced professionals, maintain open communication with employees, stay up-to-date on regulatory requirements, and regularly review and adjust your plan as needed.

Extreme Cases That Will Get You Thrown in Jail (Or Cause Otherwise Severe Penalties, Issues, or Problems for You!)

There have been IRS court cases involving issues, incorrect setups, or abuses of defined benefit plans, cash balance plans, and 401(k) plans. While it is challenging to list all cases, here are a few examples:

1. Commissioner of Internal Revenue v. Keystone Consolidated Industries, Inc. (508 U.S. 152, 1993)

In this case, the Supreme Court ruled that the company's use of its own stock to fund its defined benefit pension plan violated the tax code because the stock was not a qualifying employer security. This resulted in the disqualification of the plan and tax consequences for the company.

2. Hughes Aircraft Co. v. Jacobson (525 U.S. 432, 1999)

This case involved employees who claimed that their employer had improperly used surplus pension plan assets to pay for plan amendments that benefited only certain employees. The Supreme Court held that the company's actions did not violate ERISA because the plan was still adequately funded.

3. Lockheed Corporation v. Spink (517 U.S. 882, 1996)

The Supreme Court ruled that an employer did not violate its fiduciary duties under ERISA by amending its pension plan to provide additional benefits to certain employees who agreed to early retirement.

4. Enron Corp. Savings Plan v. Hewitt Associates L.L.C. (2006)

In this case, Enron's 401(k) plan participants sued the plan administrator, claiming that it breached its fiduciary duty by not preventing the employees from investing in Enron stock. The court held that the plan administrator did not have a fiduciary duty to override the investment options offered by the plan.

These cases illustrate the importance of proper plan setup, compliance with regulations, and ongoing monitoring to ensure the plans are operated correctly and in the best interest of participants. Working with experienced professionals and staying current on regulatory requirements can help avoid legal issues and ensure a successful retirement plan for your business and employees.

If You Want to Know More (Bonus)

These types of programs are a combination between you, your CPA, your financial advisor, and your tax strategist. Our experts work with specialized versions of benefit plans, cash balance plans, and 401(k) plans.

These strategies offer the potential to significantly bolster your retirement savings while also providing the opportunity to convert them into tax-free income after a period of five years.

If you're seeking expert guidance and personalized assistance in implementing these strategies, we have an extensive network of trusted professionals who can provide the support you need.

So, if your CPA is not clear on your options in this arena and you want additional information, we suggest that you book a call with our team. We have a wealth of expertise and a vast network of specialists who can assist you in achieving these goals.

Selling Without Taxation: Keep ALL Your Money

❝

The old adage, 'If it sounds too good to be true, it probably is,' isn't always correct. In fact, the suspicion, cynicism, and doubt that are inherent in this belief can and does keep people from taking advantage of excellent opportunities.

—Richard Carlson

The Strategy: Section 453 and DSTs

Aggression Scale Level: 5+

Sarah and Andrew, a successful entrepreneurial couple, approached us with concerns about the substantial capital gains tax they were facing from the sale of one of their investment properties: a taxable gain of over $1.6 million. They had heard about a strategy called a "monetized installment trust," but they were skeptical, fearing that it might be too good to be true or even illegal.

As I sat down with them over Zoom, everyone's morning coffee in hand, I could see the apprehension in their eyes. They wanted to explore their options, but they needed reassurance that this strategy was both legal and effective.

"Is this monetized installment trust thing really legitimate?" Andrew asked, his brow furrowed with concern.

"Absolutely," I replied. "It's a legal strategy under Tax Code section 453 that allows you to defer your capital gains taxes and invest the funds that you would have paid in taxes. Instead of handing over 25% of your $1.6 million gain, you can use that $400k to buy another property—the one you were looking at for that new Airbnb in Florida. So instead of the IRS having your money, you can keep it and earn even more cash!"

I could see that Sarah and Andrew were still feeling uncertain, so I decided to share a story with them to illustrate the importance of being open-minded to opportunities that may seem too good to be true.

"Let me suspend your disbelief for a minute here, Sarah. Follow me for a moment," I said.

Now, I love going into story mode. I feel that things just make so much more sense with stories, so I get pretty animated—shifting forward in my chair and marking the start of the story with my hands up in exclamation.

"Once upon a time," my favorite start to any story, "A couple celebrated their 40th wedding anniversary at a fancy restaurant. During the dinner, the husband presented his wife with a beautiful, very old, gold antique locket on a chain. The couple exchanged loving glances, and the wife carefully opened the locket. To their amazement, a tiny fairy appeared before them, glowing with radiant light."

Sarah smiled, and Andrew smirked. I continued, "The fairy explained that their 40 years of devotion to each other had released her from the locket, and she could now grant them each a wish. The wife, without hesitating, wished for a round-the-world holiday with her husband, so they could continue to experience life together as they had always been—in love and happy. The fairy waved her wand, and two first-class tickets materialized before them.

"Now it was the husband's turn to make a wish. He thought for a few seconds and, with a guilty expression, wished for a younger wife so he could fully enjoy the holiday of a lifetime.

The fairy, understanding the implications of his wish, cleverly waved her wand, and the husband aged instantly, becoming 93 years old."

Sarah laughed as she looked with a side-eye at Andrew, and he threw his hands up as if to say "Not me, honey!" and smiled.

"Listen," I said slyly, smiling. "The lesson of the story is clear: sometimes opportunities that seem too good to be true are genuine, but it's crucial to approach them with care and wisdom. That's what we do—we have the care and wisdom to help you use the correct strategies for the right types of issues and taxation woes so that you can go on your dream vacation together without one of you turning 93!"

Andrew laughed.

Sarah hesitated, and said, "We've worked so hard to build our wealth, and we want to protect it. How can we be sure that this strategy won't backfire on us?"

I smiled reassuringly. "I understand your concerns, and we're here to make sure everything is done correctly. Our team will guide you through each step, ensuring that you're following the tax laws properly."

Our team of tax experts spent hours with Sarah and Andrew, pouring over tax code section 453 and case studies of monetized installment trusts. We walked them through the process, ensuring they understood every step and the legality of the strategy.

Gradually, Sarah and Andrew's skepticism began to fade. They started to see the potential benefits of using a monetized installment trust to defer their capital gains tax and grow their investments. With our guidance, they decided to implement the strategy, confident in the legality and effectiveness of the approach.

Let me give you one of my examples of using legal tax strategies to your advantage.

Apple, the tech giant, has been a master at employing tax strategies to reduce its annual tax burden. They have taken advantage of tax laws in various countries to minimize their taxes, much to the chagrin of many governments. One of the most famous tax strategies Apple employed involved forming companies in Ireland and the British Virgin Islands. This method, known as the "Double Irish with a Dutch Sandwich" strategy, allowed Apple to funnel profits through these countries and leverage their favorable tax laws.

Ireland had a corporate tax rate of 12.5%, significantly lower than the U.S. rate. However, Apple went even further, negotiating a special deal with the Irish government that allowed them to pay an effective tax rate of less than 2%.[1] In addition to the Irish subsidiaries, Apple established a shell company in the British Virgin Islands, a known tax haven. By funneling profits through this shell company, Apple was able to avoid paying taxes on billions of dollars of revenue.

---

[1] Ap, "Apple Only Paid 1.9% Tax on Foreign Earnings of $37 Billion Last Year," Business Insider, November 5, 2012, https://www.businessinsider.com/apple-tax-rate-2012-11#:~:text=Apple%20Inc.,the%20fiscal%20year%20ended%20Sept.

The "Double Irish with a Dutch Sandwich" strategy worked as follows: Apple transferred its intellectual property rights, such as patents and trademarks, to its Irish subsidiary. This subsidiary then licensed these rights to another Irish company, which was managed from the low-tax jurisdiction of the British Virgin Islands. The second Irish company then sublicensed these rights to a Dutch subsidiary. The Dutch subsidiary received royalties from Apple's global sales and transferred them to the first Irish company, which, in turn, paid the second Irish company as a deductible expense. This intricate process allowed Apple to minimize its tax liabilities significantly.

Although this strategy has been criticized and has since been phased out, it is a prime example of how a company can legally use existing tax laws to its advantage. These strategies are not inherently illegal or immoral; they simply involve leveraging the tax codes of different jurisdictions to maximize profit and minimize tax burdens.

Months later, Sarah, Andrew, and I hopped on a check-in call.

"We couldn't be happier, Shauna, this installment trust is amazing," said Sarah, her face beaming with gratitude. "By setting this up, not only were we able to defer the $1.6 million gain from our original deal, but we've since integrated three more sales, so now our trust has over $4 million completely deferred in it, growing and making us money!" She was almost jumping out of her chair, giddy with excitement. "We've got everything we wanted and more—AND—we're taking a trip around the world with the tax savings! But no 93-year-old husband for me," she laughed. "Andrew will do just fine!"

By implementing the monetized installment trust strategy,

they had legally deferred their capital gains taxes, allowing the funds they would have paid in taxes to grow and work for them instead. They could now focus on expanding their business and enjoying their hard-earned success.

"Thank you so much for guiding us through this process," Sarah said, her eyes shining with gratitude. "We couldn't have done it without your expertise and support."

In conclusion, while skepticism can sometimes protect us from scams, it can also prevent us from benefiting from legitimate opportunities. Understanding and utilizing tax strategies like monetized installment trusts can help savvy individuals and businesses legally minimize their tax burdens and make the most of their financial resources.

Just like the couple in the fairy story, it's essential to approach opportunities with an open mind, but also with care and wisdom. By doing so, and with the help of trusted experts, you may discover that what initially seemed "too good to be true" can become a reality that positively impacts your financial future. Embrace the potential of legal tax strategies, and watch your wealth and success grow.

The Implementation

A Monetized Installment Sale (MIS), sometimes called a Monetized Installment Trust, is a tax strategy that allows you to defer capital gains tax on the sale of an appreciated asset. The strategy involves a combination of a sale (installment or pay in full) and additional loan arrangements.

Step 1: Consult with tax and legal professionals.

Before implementing a Monetized Installment Sale, consult with tax and legal professionals to ensure that it is suitable for your situation and to get assistance in setting up the necessary arrangements. (If your CPA is not familiar with these strategies, our team would be happy to walk through the basics with you and help you if you want more detailed professional support. Just book a time with our team at **TaxGoddess.com/Growth-Team**.)

Step 2: Find a buyer for the appreciated asset.

Identify a buyer who is willing to purchase the appreciated asset, such as real estate or a business, using an installment sale agreement or pay in full.

Step 3: Set up an intermediary.

An intermediary, often a trust or a specialized entity, is needed to facilitate the transaction. The intermediary will enter into an installment or pay-in-full sale agreement with the buyer and a loan agreement with you, the seller. Note that if the seller pays in full, you will negotiate an agreement with the trust/intermediary for payments to you on a note (as you, the seller, sold an asset to the trust/intermediary and you expect a payment with interest for the asset you sold).

Step 4: Complete the sale.

The buyer will purchase the asset from the intermediary using either an installment sale agreement or they will pay in full to the intermediary. At this point, there are two different options depending on the sale (paid in full or installment payments).

FOR AN INSTALLMENT SALE:

Step 5: Obtain a monetization loan.

Simultaneously with the installment sale, you will obtain a monetization loan from a lender, usually a bank or financial institution. The loan amount is typically a percentage (e.g., 90-95%) of the asset's sale price. The loan is secured by the installment sale agreement between the intermediary and the buyer.

Step 6: Receive loan proceeds.

You will receive the loan proceeds from the monetization loan, which provides you with immediate liquidity without triggering capital gains tax, as the loan is not considered a taxable event.

Step 7: Buyer makes installment payments.

The buyer will make installment payments to the intermediary according to the agreed-upon schedule. These payments will include principal and interest.

Step 8: Intermediary makes loan payments.

The intermediary will use the buyer's installment payments to make loan payments to the lender. The loan payments will also include principal and interest.

Step 9: Pay off the loan and receive remaining installment payments.

When the monetization loan is fully repaid, you will begin to receive any remaining installment payments from the intermediary. At this point, you will recognize capital gains and pay taxes on the installment payments received.

IF PAY IN FULL:

Step 5: The intermediary receives cash.

The intermediary will receive the full amount of the cash from the sale, and will invest these funds to be able to repay its note due to you, the seller.

Step 6: Receive payments on your loan with the intermediary/trust.

You, the seller, will receive payments from the intermediary/trust. At this point, you will recognize capital gains and pay taxes on the installment payments received.

Keep in mind that this is a complex tax strategy, and it's crucial to work with experienced tax and legal professionals to properly set up and execute a Monetized Installment Sale. Laws and regulations may change over time, so always consult with professionals to stay up-to-date on current rules and best practices.

The Pitfalls

Monetized Installment Sales are complex transactions that must be carefully structured and managed to avoid potential pitfalls. Here are some common issues that can cause problems with an MIS:

- Improper structuring: The MIS must be structured correctly to meet IRS guidelines. Any missteps in the structuring of the deal, such as the buyer and seller not dealing at arm's length or the monetization loan not being set up properly, could trigger immediate tax consequences.

- Failure to meet IRS requirements: If the IRS determines that the transaction does not meet the requirements for an installment sale under Section 453 of the Internal Revenue Code, you could owe taxes immediately on the entire gain from the sale.

- Buyer default: If the buyer defaults on their installment payments, this could potentially leave the intermediary unable to repay the loan, which could cause financial losses and potential tax liabilities.

- Changes in tax laws: Tax laws and regulations can change, potentially affecting the benefits of an MIS. For example, changes in capital gains tax rates or installment sale rules could impact the tax consequences of an MIS.

- Legal and regulatory risk: There's some uncertainty surrounding the legal and regulatory status of MIS transactions. The IRS has not specifically approved or disapproved of these transactions, and future court cases or IRS guidance could impact their viability.

- Loan risks: There's a risk that the terms of the monetization loan could change over time, such as an increase in interest rates, which could affect the profitability of the transaction.

- Market risks: Changes in the value of the asset sold or in the broader economic environment could affect the buyer's ability to make installment payments, potentially leading to a default.

- Intermediary risk: If the intermediary fails or becomes insolvent, this could disrupt the transaction and potentially lead to tax consequences.

Given these potential pitfalls, it's crucial to work with experienced tax professionals and legal advisors when setting up and managing a Monetized Installment Sale. They can help you navigate these complexities and mitigate potential risks.

Extreme Cases That Will Get You Thrown in Jail (Or Cause Otherwise Severe Penalties, Issues, or Problems for You!)

One of the most famous recent cases of "it's too good to be true" was the Wesley Snipes case.

Wesley Snipes, a famous American actor, became entangled in legal trouble in 2006 when he was indicted on multiple charges related to tax evasion. Snipes, along with his co-defendants Eddie Ray Kahn and Douglas P. Rosile, was accused of conspiracy to defraud the United States, filing false claims for tax refunds and failing to file federal income tax returns.

Snipes was a proponent of the "tax protester" movement, which contends that the federal income tax system is illegal or unconstitutional. Under the guidance of Kahn, who founded the American Rights Litigators and Guiding Light of God Ministries, and Rosile, an accountant, Snipes participated in a scheme to defraud the IRS. They allegedly prepared and submitted fraudulent amended tax returns on Snipes' behalf, claiming refunds totaling nearly $12 million. In reality, Snipes owed millions of dollars in taxes.

In addition to the conspiracy and fraud charges, Snipes faced allegations of not filing tax returns for the years 1999 through 2004, even though he earned substantial income during that time. His income was estimated to be around $38 million.

In 2008, after a high-profile trial, Snipes was acquitted of the more serious conspiracy and fraud charges but was convicted of three misdemeanor counts for willfully failing to file federal income tax returns. He was sentenced to three years in prison, the maximum penalty for these misdemeanor convictions, to serve as a deterrent to others who might consider evading taxes. Snipes began serving his sentence in December 2010 and was released in April 2013.

After his release, Snipes still faced the issue of unpaid taxes. Although the exact amount owed was contested, in November 2018, the United States Tax Court ruled that Snipes had to pay the IRS nearly $9.5 million in back taxes, interest, and penalties. The court determined that Snipes had failed to show reasonable cause for not filing accurate tax returns and that his reliance on the advice of Kahn and Rosile was not reasonable.

It is crucial to thoroughly investigate the strategies you plan to apply to your financial circumstances. Verify that the professionals you engage to assist you possess extensive experience implementing these strategies for numerous clients over an extended period. Additionally, confirm that they have demonstrated successful audit records associated with the implementation of these strategies.

If You Want to Know More (BONUS)

This particular strategy is SO complicated that I have actually filmed a webinar dedicated to this subject.

So, if you are "selling something big" and want to know how to NOT pay taxes on the sale, we suggest that you watch my webinar:

DST4Me.com

This webinar and website will walk you through the details, help you run calculations on exactly how much you can save, and ensure that you have the proper team to help you do this right.

After all, a BIG sale doesn't happen every day, so ensuring that it's all done correctly and you get to keep all your cash is pretty important!

Whatever you decide to do with your sale (business sale, real estate sale, massive stock sell-off, whatever the "big" sale is) ensure you are working with quality providers who will guide you, teach you, protect you, and handle the nitty-gritty to make the deal perfect.

The $190,000 "Oopsie"

> Alone, we can do so little; together, we can do so much.
>
> —Helen Keller

The Strategy: Proper Use of an Accountable Plan

Aggression Scale Level: -2 (Every CPA should know this and more than 50% MISS THIS ONE!)

"I'm sorry … what?! I can pay myself HOW MUCH for using my personal vehicle for business purposes?" Jamie said incredulously.

Jamie's face was one that I had seen many, many times before. Pushed forward on his seat, eyebrows raised, jaw hitting the floor.

You see, I had just told Jamie that based on the fact that he was using his personal vehicle for business purposes, he should be able to write off a significant amount of expenses from his business using an accountable plan.

"My guys never told me that," Jamie mumbled, his eyes dissatisfied and his lips pursed in disappointment.

An accountable plan is one of the most commonly underused, commonly best, and most expensive mistakes your CPA will ever make. An accountable plan is a pre-IRS-approved tax-saving tool used by businesses to reimburse employees for work-related expenses while ensuring that the reimbursement remains tax-free.

By implementing an accountable plan, a company can properly deduct certain personal expenses paid on behalf of the business, ultimately benefiting both the employer and the employee.

There are various expenses that can be covered under an accountable plan. These include business travel expenses, such as transportation, lodging, and meals; supplies and materials required for work; and even the cost of using an employee's personal vehicle for business purposes. Additionally, an accountable plan can cover expenses related to home office usage, professional development courses, and membership fees for industry associations.

To effectively track expenses under an accountable plan, it is crucial to maintain accurate and organized records. This involves collecting receipts and invoices for all reimbursed expenses, as well as documenting the specific business purpose for each expenditure.

Staff and owners alike should submit expense reports on a regular basis, providing details such as the date, amount, and nature of the expense.

By keeping thorough records and adhering to the plan's guidelines, businesses can ensure compliance with IRS regulations and make the most of this valuable tax strategy.

I was floored. I couldn't believe that Jamie had never even heard the term accountable plan, let alone didn't have one.

I swear this is one of those things that just riles my feathers as a tax strategist. An accountable plan in my mind is not so much even a strategy as it is a baseline deduction that every CPA should take for every client. Period.

I was not looking forward to calculating how much and for how many years Jamie's CPA had been overtaxing when we ran the final calculations on the accountable plan. Jamie would be devastated!

Jamie is a successful business owner, operating three construction-related companies (an HVAC company, a plumbing contractor, and an electrical contractor). He had always done very well, and his best friend Sam, who referred Jamie to us, had of course spoken about how happy he was with our team and the work we did for him.

Jamie and I were on our standard "get-to-know-you" Zoom call, and he was describing his three businesses. He told us about his crews, his profit margins, how his businesses refer clients between them, and how the cross-marketing has really helped him corner his market in Philly.

The passion and enthusiasm that Jamie had for his businesses were tangible. Even though we were on a Zoom call, Jamie was wildly gesturing, his tone and inflection consistently going up and down based on what he was describing. It's always nice to see somebody so zealous about their business; a true sign of someone who loves what they do.

Jamie's business was highly successful, and between the three companies, he was taking home about $850,000 per year.

For Jamie, as for many other business owners, one of the most important principles to understand is that every business owner needs a strong, reliable team by their side.

The success of any venture hinges on the collective effort and expertise of individuals who can execute even the most complex strategies with precision and efficiency.

When you have a plan, a checklist, and a team that supports and empowers you, the possibilities for growth are limitless.

Having a dedicated team not only helps in implementing strategies but also provides a sense of stability and confidence in your decision-making process. Your team can help you navigate the ever-changing landscape of business, offering their expertise and guidance when you face challenges or opportunities.

Together, you can tackle obstacles head-on and continuously strive for improvement, knowing that you are backed by a group of professionals committed to your success.

This principle is the foundation of a thriving enterprise, and when embraced, it can propel your business to new heights.

I leaned back in my chair, took a breath, and with an empathetic expression, I gently asked Jamie, "So, tell me about your current relationship with your CPA."

Jamie's entire demeanor shifted to one of dejection. His shoulders slumped, and a flash of anger flickered in his eyes. With a scowl and a slow shake of his head, he began to speak. "I am so fed up with those guys. About three weeks ago, I gave them a

THE $190,000 "OOPSIE"

call and an email and requested a meeting over the voicemail that I left to discuss the level of service that I'm receiving. I said in the voicemail that if I don't get a call back within 48 hours, our relationship is effectively over. It's been three weeks. I'm just done."

I furrowed my brow and nodded. There's not much you can say about this to someone. This is such a common complaint; we hear it at least five times a week. Today's CPA firms are understaffed and overworked. Clients like Jamie thought they had a strong relationship with their CPA, someone they could rely on. But the CPA didn't even have the time to return a simple telephone call.

Jamie went on to explain, "As my businesses have become more successful, I need more guidance. I have more questions, more situations that come up, and I need more attention from my CPA—not less! It's so frustrating when you need an answer to a simple question or ask for a return phone call, and no one even bothers to respond."

Having a team that you can rely on is crucial—a team that will provide guidance when you need it, a team that gets you answers to your questions (and doesn't just say "I don't know" or "I'll get back to you" and never does!).

Think about it this way:

English playwright John Haywood said that "Rome wasn't built in a day, but they were laying bricks every hour."[2]

---

[2] Bill Yeargin, "Musings of a CEO - Trade Only Today," Musings of a CEO, May

This is a reminder that it requires time, patience, relationships, communication, and teamwork to create something great.

When Rome was being built across its vast territory, spanning an area of over 23,000,000 mi.² over three continents—Africa, Asia, and Europe—it is estimated that perhaps 60 million people lived within its borders.

In order to build an empire of this magnitude, the leadership of Rome required not only military dominance but also political, economic, social, and religious expansion that would allow it to expand from one of the many city-states in the Italian peninsula to being the center of the most powerful empire in the world.

In order to build the empire, Rome needed not only the Emperor but also military generals, tax collectors, financiers, priests, artists, merchants, supervisors, farmers, etc.

It is very similar in today's world in any successful business organization. In order to expand, grow, and steal market share from other empires, you need teams, divisions, managers, leaders, and workers across many divisions of the business (sales, marketing, finance, production, operations, etc.).

Jamie had all of these things. Across his three companies, his staff was over 120 people in a wide variety of departments, implementing a wide variety of systems.

Jamie's need for communication and guidance was simple, and

2, 2022, https://www.tradeonlytoday.com/manufacturers/musings-of-a-ceo.

yet, he was always frustrated—left out in the cold.

Jamie had built an amazing empire, but one of the key players in his team was missing in action. Without the guidance of his CPA, he was unable to make financial decisions that would impact his entire organization. Sometimes these decisions and questions are simple things, like deciding whether to implement an accountable plan for reimbursing employee expenses. Sometimes these things are much more intense, detailed, and complicated—like whether to buy that small business and bring in their crew to join yours as part of a merger and acquisition.

If you make the wrong decision based on inaccurate or untimely information, it can be life or death for a business.

Without a team at Jamie's back, his business could make serious missteps that could cause a demise similar to the fall of the Roman Empire.

"I just need a team that picks up the phone when I call them. When I have a question, I need an answer. I need guidance. I need to know that my company is as much of a priority to my CPA as it is to me, and right now, I am not feeling it," Jamie sighed, his disappointment clearly written all over his face.

After a moment, giving Jamie a chance to catch his breath and recompose himself, I looked at him seriously and asked, "So Jamie, let me make sure I understand you correctly. Your current CPA is not only not returning your telephone calls and not giving you timely guidance, but also has not been explaining the basics like an accountable plan to you?

"I have to ask, if you had a team that would reply to you within three hours of any question, if your team was available for meetings within a two-day timeframe; if the team brought YOU strategies rather than you asking for help; if when you asked a question, your team did the research and came back to you with the appropriate guidance, checklists, written research, and/or backup documentation needed; and most importantly, if you felt like your CPA had your back whenever you needed them, would this be the kind of relationship that you're looking for?"

Jamie sat up straight in his seat, looked straight into the camera, and in a very serious and powerful tone said, "Yes."

It was then that Jamie became a client of Tax Goddess.

Within the first month of our relationship, we found over $190,000 that had not been properly reported on his accountable plan. The accountable plan strategy alone, being properly implemented on his account, was able to reduce Jamie's taxes by over $76,000 per year. Better yet, we were able to go back three years (to recapture the missed deductions) and amend returns to get a little over $228,000 in cold hard cash that he had overpaid.

Jamie's team has since grown to over 273 people. He now owns two additional businesses, one real estate construction and rehab company, and, of all things, an ice cream shop. The team at Tax Goddess has helped him through the easy decisions (buying his new F350 truck) and the complex negotiations of the merger and acquisition of the two new businesses.

THE $190,000 "OOPSIE"

Jamie's management team has grown to rely on their hand-picked professional team within Tax Goddess. They now have a one-on-one relationship with their Sr. Tax Strategist, Sr. Tax Professional, Sr. Bookkeeper, Payroll Rep, and as their main point of contact, their Sr. Account Manager, who knows their entire file inside and out and has an assistant of her own to ensure continuity of knowledge, information, and previously obtained customer knowledge.

The success of Jamie's business transformation serves as a powerful reminder of the importance of having a strong, supportive team behind every business owner.

With the right guidance, expertise, and collaborative approach, even the most intricate strategies can be executed with precision and efficiency.

The key to unlocking the full potential of any business lies in the synergy between the business owner and their chosen team of professionals. Together, they can address challenges, make informed decisions, and drive the business toward new heights.

In Jamie's case, the Tax Goddess team played an instrumental role in implementing the accountable plan strategy, which not only saved him a significant amount in taxes but also enabled his businesses to thrive and expand.

This highlights the impact of having a dedicated team that is committed to understanding the unique needs of a business and working tirelessly to support its growth.

As the story of Jamie and his Tax Goddess team demonstrates, the foundation for lasting success is built on collaboration, trust, and the unwavering commitment of a team that shares a common vision.

I was lucky enough to meet with Jamie a few weeks back and this story came up:

"You know, Shauna, after the terrible experience I had with that old CPA, I never knew that there was someone like you and your team out there. Someone who actually cares about what happens to my business as much as I do and is willing to help me get things done."

I couldn't have felt more proud and heart-warmed that we gave Jamie what he desperately needed and wanted—a true partner.

To build an empire, you need a team, guidance, and support. If you don't have that now, what's holding you back?

Jamie's story is not unique. Many business owners struggle with finding the right team of professionals to support their vision and help them grow. If you find yourself in a similar situation, it's time to evaluate your current relationships and consider whether it's time to make a change.

Seek out a team of professionals who understand your industry, share your passion for growth, and prioritize communication and responsiveness. Surround yourself with experts who can guide you through the complexities of business, tax, and financial decisions, and help you avoid costly mistakes.

Your empire is waiting to be built, and the right team can help you achieve greatness. Don't settle for less than you deserve; find a team that truly has your back, and together, you can accomplish great things.

> **"**
> Coming together is a beginning, staying together is progress, and working together is success.
>
> —Henry Ford

The Implementation

An accountable plan is a reimbursement arrangement between an employer and employees that adheres to the IRS guidelines, allowing reimbursed expenses to be excluded from the employee's taxable income. Here's a step-by-step guide on setting up and maintaining an accountable plan from both the business and staff perspectives.

BUSINESS PERSPECTIVE:

Step 1: Familiarize yourself with IRS guidelines.

Review IRS Publication 463 and familiarize yourself with the requirements for an accountable plan, which includes a business connection, substantiation, and returning excess reimbursements.

Step 2: Draft a written accountable plan.

Create a written document outlining the accountable plan policies, including the types of expenses covered, the reimbursement process, documentation requirements, and deadlines for submitting expenses and returning excess reimbursements.

Step 3: Establish expense categories.

Determine the types of expenses eligible for reimbursement under the accountable plan, such as travel, meals, and business supplies.

Step 4: Set reimbursement rates.

Establish reimbursement rates for different expense categories. For example, use the IRS standard mileage rate for reimbursing employees' use of their personal vehicles for business purposes.

Step 5: Communicate the plan to employees.

Distribute the accountable plan document to all employees and provide training on the policies and procedures.

Step 6: Implement a reimbursement process.

Set up a system for employees to submit expense reports and documentation, and designate a person or department responsible for reviewing and approving reimbursements.

Step 7: Review and approve expenses.

Review submitted expense reports for compliance with the accountable plan policies, and approve or deny reimbursements accordingly.

Step 8: Maintain thorough records.

Keep accurate records of all expense reports, receipts, and reimbursements for a minimum of three years, as required by the IRS.

Step 9: Monitor the plan for compliance.

Regularly review the accountable plan's effectiveness and adherence to IRS guidelines, and update the policies as needed to maintain compliance.

STAFF PERSPECTIVE:

Step 1: Understand the accountable plan.

Review the accountable plan document provided by your employer and familiarize yourself with the policies, procedures, and eligible expenses.

Step 2: Incur expenses with a business connection.

Only seek reimbursement for expenses with a direct business connection, such as those necessary for performing your job duties.

Step 3. Retain documentation.

Keep receipts and other documentation for all reimbursable expenses, including the date, amount, and business purpose of each expense.

Step 4: Complete expense reports.

Fill out expense reports according to your employer's policies, providing all required information and documentation.

Step 5: Submit expense reports promptly.

Submit expense reports within the time frame specified in the accountable plan, typically within 60 days of incurring the expense.

Step 6: Return excess reimbursements.

If you receive a reimbursement that exceeds your substantiated expenses, promptly return the excess amount to your employer within the accountable plan's specified time frame, typically 120 days.

By following these steps, both businesses and staff can ensure that an accountable plan is properly set up and maintained, allowing for tax-free reimbursements and compliance with IRS guidelines.

The Pitfalls

When writing, using, or implementing an accountable plan, there are several potential pitfalls and mistakes that people might encounter:

- Failing to create a written plan: THIS IS THE BIG ONE. NO DEDUCTIONS FOR YOU IF YOU HAVE NO PLAN! It's important to have a written accountable plan that clearly outlines the policies and procedures. A lack of written documentation could lead to misunderstandings, errors, and difficulties proving the plan's existence during an IRS audit.

- Inadequate communication with employees: Employers must ensure that employees are aware of the accountable plan and its requirements. Ineffective communication can result in employees not following the plan's guidelines, which may lead to disallowed reimbursements or increased taxable income.

- Insufficient documentation: Both employees and employers must keep accurate records of all reimbursed expenses. Failing to maintain proper documentation can make it difficult to substantiate expenses during an IRS audit and may result in denied reimbursements or tax penalties.

- Not meeting the IRS requirements: An accountable plan must meet three key requirements: a business connection, substantiation, and returning excess reimbursements. Failing to meet any of these requirements can lead to the plan being deemed nonaccountable, which can result in increased taxable income for employees and possible tax penalties for the employer.

- Inconsistent application of plan rules: Employers must apply the rules of the accountable plan consistently to all employees. Inconsistent application can lead to confusion, errors, and potential issues with the IRS.

- Missing deadlines: Employees must submit expense reports and return excess reimbursements within the specified time frames outlined in the accountable plan. Missing these deadlines can result in expense reimbursements being considered taxable income.

- Mixing personal and business expenses: Employees must ensure that reimbursed expenses have a legitimate business connection. Mixing personal and business expenses can lead to denied reimbursements and potential tax issues.

- Failing to regularly review and update the plan: Tax laws and regulations can change over time, and employers should periodically review and update their accountable plan to ensure ongoing compliance with IRS guidelines.

By being aware of these potential pitfalls and mistakes, both employers and employees can take steps to avoid them and ensure the successful implementation and maintenance of an accountable plan.

Extreme Cases That Will Get You Thrown in Jail (Or Cause Otherwise Severe Penalties, Issues, or Problems for You!)

While an accountable plan is designed to provide tax-free reimbursements for legitimate business expenses, it could be misused or abused in several ways, potentially leading to tax fraud or noncompliance issues. Some examples include:

1. Overstating expenses: Employees might exaggerate or falsify the cost of business expenses in order to receive larger reimbursements than they are entitled to. This could lead to the employee receiving an unjust tax benefit.

2. Claiming personal expenses as business expenses: Employees may attempt to claim personal expenses as business-related in order to receive tax-free reimbursements. This could include expenses that have no direct connection to their job duties or that are not necessary for conducting business.

3. Inflating mileage or travel costs: Employees could overstate their mileage or travel expenses to receive larger reimbursements. This might involve logging more miles than actually driven or submitting travel expenses for personal trips.

4. Failing to return excess reimbursements: Employees might neglect to return excess reimbursements within the required

time frame, effectively converting those funds into unreported taxable income.

5. Fabricating expenses: In extreme cases, employees could create entirely fictitious expenses, submitting false receipts or expense reports in order to receive reimbursements.

6. Collusion between employees and employers: Employers and employees could collude to use the accountable plan as a way to provide additional tax-free compensation, intentionally disregarding the plan's requirements and documentation standards.

7. Ignoring IRS guidelines: Employers might not follow IRS guidelines for accountable plans, leading to noncompliant practices that could expose both the employer and employees to potential tax penalties and legal consequences.

To prevent misuse or abuse of an accountable plan, it is essential for employers to establish clear guidelines, maintain proper documentation, and regularly review the plan's effectiveness and compliance. Additionally, employees should be educated about the plan's rules and requirements, as well as the consequences of misusing or abusing the system.

If You Want to Know More (BONUS)

We want to ensure you are covered with this strategy. It "seems" easy, but CPAs misuse this strategy over 50% of the time, and I don't want you to be the one that has it done wrong (and have the IRS take away your deductions).

Items you need:

Video instruction on accountable plans:
bit.ly/AcctPlanVid

Accountable plan document link:
bit.ly/AcctPlanDoc

Get your Income & Expense Tracker here:
TaxGoddess.com/Income-Expense-Tracker

Customizable Accountable Plan Calculation Tool:
TaxGoddess.com/Accountable-Plan-Calculation-Tool

Book your Review Call with our team to ensure you've done this right:
TaxGoddess.com/SixLifeCheck

As you know, in *The 6% Life*, I have crafted the tax strategies to be timeless. We have not provided a tracking mechanism (as the rates change yearly), so please work with your CPA using their tracking mechanism.

We know that not everyone wants to do this on their own, so if you don't feel comfortable or your CPA tells you "No, I won't sign off on that," or worse yet, your CPA seems totally unaware that you can even do this, then book a free consultation with us at **TaxGoddess.com/Growth-Team** so we can become your new (and improved) CPA team!

Time Is Money, Money Is Time

> Time is a created thing.
> To say 'I don't have time'
> is to say 'I don't want to.'
>
> —Lao Tzu[3]

---

[3] Lao Tzu was a Chinese philosopher and writer who lived during the 6th century BC, and is considered the founder of Taoism. Lao Tzu is known for his book, the *Tao Te Ching*, which is a fundamental text of Taoist philosophy. The *Tao Te Ching* is a collection of verses that provide guidance on various aspects of life, including leadership, morality, and personal conduct. Some historical texts also attribute a book on military strategy called the *Tao of War*, also known as *The Art of War*, to Lao Tzu, which is a treatise on warfare that provides advice on tactics, strategy, and leadership.

The Strategy: Infinite Banking & Premium Financing

Aggression Scale Level: 1

Lao Tzu, one of the most famous ancient Chinese military strategists and founder of Taoism, suggests that saying "I don't have time" is actually a choice not to prioritize a particular task or goal. He encourages individuals to take ownership of their time and make conscious decisions about how they spend it, rather than simply blaming their busy schedules. In the context of tax strategy, it implies that not taking the time to consider tax planning may be a choice, rather than a true lack of time.

His theories are globally implemented and still come into play even in the day-to-day lives of regular citizens. Consider the story of Jack and Michelle.

The sun cast warm rays of light through the large windows of Michelle's home office, throwing a golden glow upon her sleek wooden desk and the many books lining her floor-to-ceiling shelves. The lush green leaves of the trees outside seemed to dance in the gentle breeze, creating a serene backdrop for her work.

However, as always, Michelle sat at her desk, furiously typing away on her laptop. As a successful entrepreneur, she was constantly juggling multiple projects and responsibilities. Her calendar was filled with meetings, deadlines, and networking events, leaving her little time for anything else. She didn't even have a moment to glance at the beauty that was surrounding her.

As she finished the email that she was so focused on, she glanced up from her screen and took a moment to look around her spacious home office, designed and built by her loving husband, Jack, as a surprise for their fifth wedding anniversary. The room was a testament to their shared love of learning and growth, but also a reminder of the importance of balance in life. Michelle loved her work, but she also knew that she needed more time to spend with Jack and their two young children, Lily and Noah.

That evening, after tucking the kids into bed, Michelle and Jack were sitting on the couch, sipping on glasses of red wine as they discussed their financial goals. They wanted to ensure their children's education was taken care of and that they could retire comfortably, but they also wanted more time together as a family.

Jack said, "You've been working too much honey. I really want to help you relax a bit and be able to spend some quality time with me and the kids."

"I know," said Michelle, "I wish that too honey. But you know how it is. I've got to work hard now. There are so many things to pay for, and so many goals that we have. If I don't really push it now, we won't be able to do the things we want to later—the kids' college has to be funded, and retirement?!

That's a laugh if we have to keep paying the taxes we are now. We won't ever have the money to retire. We will both be working until we are 80!"

"Well," Jack said, "Jim at work told me about his tax strategy team—people over at the Tax Goddess. He said that they set up this special type of retirement plan that will give him completely tax-free retirement money for him and his wife, and can be used to pay for the kids' college tax-free as well. Maybe we should check them out?"

Michelle sighed, exasperated, and shook her head. "We already have retirement accounts, Jack. How is some other type of retirement going to help? It's all taxable in the end anyway! I've never seen retirement that isn't taxable other than a Roth account, and we make too much money for that. So what's the point? I want more time with you and the kids now. I don't want to work harder to just hand over even more money in taxes. I just don't have the time to add one more thing on top of my plate."

Jack laughed lovingly. "Hun, I can tell you are stressed. You missed an important word here: TAX-FREE! This retirement is 100% tax-free for life, forever, meaning no taxes and no working harder to make up for lost tax funds. And it's tax-free assets for our kids when we die."

Michelle caught herself and laughed a little. "Oh geez, sorry. You're right. I'm just way too stressed out. Listen, if this works well for Jim, let's go talk to these people and see what they can do for us."

That's when they decided to consult with our team and change their lives forever.

During their first meeting with us, we introduced them to the concept of Infinite Banking—a strategy that uses whole life insurance to create a personal bank from which you can pull money tax-free to do anything you wish. Intrigued, they learned that this approach could help them buy real estate, build a business, pay for the kids' college, fund their retirement, and much more, all while being completely tax-free for life.

Most importantly, implementation of the Infinite Banking strategy will not add any additional stress, time, work, or frustration to Michelle's already crazy schedule. We actually determined that Michelle would be able to reduce her workload by about six hours a week for the rest of her working career at her current earnings level, and it would be able to fund the amounts into retirement that they wanted. She was able to actually work less, spend time with her family, and focus on what was truly important to her simply by changing the tools and strategies that they were using in their financial portfolio (by adding Infinite Banking).

Michelle couldn't help but think of Ferris Bueller's famous quote from the movie *Ferris Bueller's Day Off*. "Life moves pretty fast. If you don't stop and look around once in a while, you could miss it." Just like Ferris Bueller, who seized the day by playing hooky and exploring Chicago with his friends, Michelle knew she had to make time for what was truly important in her life. The Infinite Banking strategy seemed like the perfect solution to help her family achieve their financial goals while still making time for one another.

Excited about the prospect of Infinite Banking, Michelle and Jack decided to delve deeper. They spent about eight hours with Tax Goddess's tax strategy specialists, answering questions and learning everything they could about the approach. With the guidance and expertise of the Tax Goddess team, they began implementing the Infinite Banking strategy.

As they put this plan into action, they discovered that the whole life insurance policy would serve as a personal bank, allowing them to borrow against the cash value of the policy at any time. This would provide them with the financial flexibility to pursue various investments and opportunities without being tied down to traditional loans and their accompanying interest rates.

Not only was Michelle saving the six hours per week that she no longer had to work, but Jack was able to use the funds inside Infinite Banking to buy some real estate properties to create additional passive income for the family!

Over time, Michelle and Jack's decision to work with Tax Goddess and implement the Infinite Banking strategy paid off tremendously. They were able to generate over $250,000 per year in tax-free income using the program for their retirement and investments. This newfound financial freedom and security allowed them to prioritize what was most important to them: time with their family.

As their lives transformed, Michelle and Jack said that they were reminded of the movie *50 First Dates*, in which the protagonist, played by Adam Sandler, intentionally took the time to make the woman of his dreams fall in love with him over and over again, every day, because it was important to him. Just like in the movie, Michelle and Jack chose to focus on what was truly important to them: spending more time together and creating beautiful memories with their children.

As the years went by, Michelle and Jack continued to apply the principles they learned from Tax Goddess and the Infinite Banking strategy. Their investments grew, and so did their tax-free income. This allowed them to take vacations as a family, explore new hobbies, and invest in their children's education without worrying about financial constraints.

In time, they were able to pay for Lily and Noah's college education, ensuring their children had a solid foundation for their future. And as they approached retirement, Michelle and Jack felt confident in their financial security, knowing that they had built a solid nest egg through the Infinite Banking strategy.

Every now and then, Michelle still sits in her home office, gazing out her window, remembering all the wonderful moments she was able to spend with her family. She feels a deep sense of gratitude for the wisdom and guidance provided by Tax Goddess and the implementation of the Infinite Banking strategy.

It isn't just the tax-free income or the financial security that she cherishes, but the time she was able to spend with her family. With each laugh, hug, and shared experience, she has realized the true value of time and the importance of making space for the things that truly matter in life.

Michelle and Jack's story is a testament to the power of Infinite Banking and the importance of making time for what truly matters. It's a reminder that life moves fast, and if you don't stop to appreciate the moments and invest in what's important to you, you could miss out on the true essence of living.

In the end, Michelle and Jack's journey with the Infinite Banking strategy has allowed them to create a life that is not only financially secure but also rich in love, experiences, and cherished memories. And as they look back on their lives, they know that they have made the most of their time and found the perfect balance between work, family, and pursuing their dreams.

> You make time for things that are important to you. Time is a part of your return on investment.
>
> —Anonymous

The Implementation

Step 1: Understand the Infinite Banking Concept.

First, learn about the Infinite Banking Concept (IBC). It's a strategy that uses a whole life insurance policy with a cash value component to act as a personal banking system. The policyholder can borrow against the cash value and repay the loan on their terms, creating a flexible way to save, invest, and finance their needs.

Step 2: Research providers.

Search for reputable insurance companies that offer whole life insurance policies with a cash value component. Look for online reviews, ask for recommendations from friends or family, and consult a financial advisor (that's Tax Goddess or your financial advisor) to help you find the best providers.

Step 3: Compare policies.

Gather information on different policies from multiple providers. Compare their premiums, cash value growth, loan interest rates, and any additional features like policy riders. Look for a policy that suits your financial goals and risk tolerance.

Step 4: Determine your budget.

Decide how much you can afford to pay in premiums each month. Keep in mind that a higher premium can lead to a faster-growing cash value, but you don't want to overextend yourself financially.

Step 5: Find an agent.

Contact a licensed insurance agent who specializes in whole life insurance and Infinite Banking. They will help you navigate the process, answer your questions, and provide guidance on choosing the best policy for your needs.

Step 6: Complete the application.

Fill out the application form provided by the agent. You will need to provide personal information, health history, and other details. Be honest and accurate to ensure a smooth underwriting process.

Step 7: Medical exam (if required)

Some insurance companies require a medical exam as part of the underwriting process. If required, schedule an appointment with a medical professional, who will assess your health and submit the results to the insurance company.

Step 8: Review the policy illustration.

Once the underwriting process is complete, the insurance agent will provide you with a policy illustration. This document outlines the policy's projected cash value growth, death benefit, and other details. Review it carefully and ask your agent any questions you might have.

Step 9: Sign and pay the premium.

If you're satisfied with the policy, sign the documents, and pay the initial premium. The policy will become active once the premium is paid, and you will receive your policy documents.

Step 10: Monitor and manage your policy.

Regularly review your policy and its performance. Communicate with your agent to make any adjustments as needed, such as increasing or decreasing the premium. To implement Infinite Banking, start using the cash value for loans when needed and repay them on your terms.

Remember, before implementing any financial strategy, it's essential to consult with a financial professional to ensure it aligns with your overall financial goals and risk tolerance.

The Pitfalls

- Inadequate funding: One of the biggest pitfalls with IBC is underfunding the policy. If you don't contribute enough in premiums, your policy's cash value may not grow as expected, limiting your ability to take loans and undermining the Infinite Banking strategy.

- Policy lapse: If you fail to pay your premiums on time, your policy could lapse, resulting in loss of coverage and potential tax consequences. When taking loans from your policy, ensure that you have enough cash value to cover the premiums and prevent a lapse.

- Overborrowing: Borrowing too much from the cash value could jeopardize the policy's financial stability. It's essential to keep track of your outstanding loans and maintain a reasonable loan-to-cash-value ratio to avoid overleveraging your policy.

- Poor loan repayment: Failing to repay loans in a timely manner can cause the policy's cash value to decrease and eventually lead to policy lapse. Develop a repayment plan that fits your financial situation and make sure to stick to it.

- High fees and commissions: Some whole life insurance policies come with high fees and commissions, which can eat into your cash value growth. To avoid this pitfall, research different policies, compare costs, and choose a policy with lower fees and commissions.

- Misunderstanding policy provisions: If you don't fully understand the policy provisions and features, you might make mistakes that can negatively impact the Infinite Banking strategy. Make sure to ask your agent questions and read the policy documents carefully.

- Ignoring tax implications: While loans taken from the policy's cash value are generally tax-free, certain actions, like surrendering the policy or allowing it to lapse with outstanding loans, can trigger taxable events. Consult a tax professional to understand the potential tax implications of your actions.

- Lack of diversification: Relying solely on IBC for your financial needs might expose you to risks. To mitigate these risks, consider diversifying your financial portfolio with other investment vehicles.

- Choosing the wrong provider: Selecting an unreliable or financially unstable insurance provider can put your policy at risk. Research the financial strength and reputation of potential providers to ensure the security of your investment.

- Not reviewing and updating the policy: Your financial needs and goals can change over time. Regularly review your policy to ensure it continues to align with your objectives, and make adjustments as needed.

To avoid these pitfalls, work with a knowledgeable insurance agent, educate yourself about the Infinite Banking Concept, and consult with financial and tax professionals to ensure the strategy aligns with your overall financial plan.

Extreme Cases That Will Get You Thrown in Jail (Or Cause Otherwise Severe Penalties, Issues, or Problems for You!)

There are limits to an IBC, and if you break them you end up with some pretty nasty consequences! If you surpass what's called the Modified Endowment Contract (MEC) limits on your Infinite Banking Concept (IBC) whole life insurance policy, it changes the tax treatment of the policy. MEC limits are set by the IRS to differentiate between life insurance policies and investment vehicles.

Here's what happens when a whole life insurance policy becomes a MEC:

1. Loss of tax-free loans: One of the main benefits of a non-MEC whole life insurance policy is the ability to take tax-free loans against the cash value. However, if your policy becomes an MEC, the loans taken from the cash value are no longer tax-free. Instead, the amount borrowed is treated as regular income, and you will have to pay income tax on it.

2. Tax on policy gains: The growth in cash value within a non-MEC whole life insurance policy is tax-deferred. However, if the policy becomes an MEC, any gains withdrawn from the policy (including loans) are taxed as ordinary income to the extent that there is a gain in the policy.

3. Early withdrawal penalty: If you withdraw money or take a loan from an MEC before age 59½, you may be subject to a 10% tax penalty on the taxable portion of the distribution, in addition to regular income tax.

4. Policy surrender: If you decide to surrender an MEC, the gains within the policy are taxable as ordinary income.

To avoid surpassing MEC limits, monitor your policy contributions and work with a knowledgeable insurance agent or financial professional. They can help you structure your policy to stay within the MEC limits while still maximizing the benefits of the Infinite Banking Concept.

If You Want to Know More (BONUS)

Many people are too busy to focus on what needs to be done in the present to really impact their long-term future.

They are fighting so hard to get what they want, but they aren't letting tools like Infinite Banking use the "easy" superpower of compounding to build their wealth.

They are fighting tooth and nail against taxes to try to build wealth, but sometimes taking the easy route, working with an expert who can help you get what you want (in this case, more time with your family) can get you to your goals faster, easier, and more efficiently than just trying to grind it out yourself.

We've created a guidebook on some of the most strategic implementations and uses for Infinite Banking and Premium Financing.

We want to make sure that when you take advantage of a great opportunity you are able to use all the tricks, tactics, and strategies to massively increase your wealth, flexibility, and family protection.

You can download our Tactics of Infinite Banking Guide here:

TaxGoddess.com/IBTactics

We know that not everyone wants to do this on their own, so if you don't feel comfortable doing this on your own or your CPA tells you, "Oh no! Insurance is bad," or worse yet, your CPA seems totally unaware that you can even do this, then book a free consultation with us:

TaxGoddess.com/Growth-Team

As usual, there are good and bad people out there! To safeguard yourself, it is crucial to work with reputable providers when employing this strategy.

This strategy should be implemented within a comprehensive plan; the provided details are generally applicable and may not cover all circumstances. Additionally, if you have any inquiries regarding the additional bonus information, feel free to schedule a chat with our team.

$175K Tax-Free Every Year

❝

Our goals can only be reached through the vehicle of a plan. There is no other road to success.

—Pablo Picasso

The Strategy: The Masters Exemption (AKA The Augusta Rule)

Aggression Scale Level: 3+

Victor, the owner of a thriving security services company, reached out to us with a sense of urgency. He had been grappling with the high taxes that his business incurred (over 46%), and Victor was desperate to find a solution. As we chatted in our first virtual meeting, I could see the worry etched on Victor's face.

"So, let me get this straight," Victor said, his brow furrowed in concentration. "You're saying that my business can pay me rent for using my home for company events? And that income would be tax-free for me and a deduction for the business?"

I nodded. "Exactly, Victor. The Masters Exemption allows your business to rent your home for up to 14 days per year, tax-free. The key is to ensure that you document the business purpose for each event and maintain proper records."

Victor found himself trapped in one of the most treacherous traps that can ensnare a business owner: the abyss of ignorance.

This same issue has plagued man for centuries—not knowing the truth and the options will kill you.

The story of Louis Pasteur and his discovery of germ theory serves as a powerful reminder of the importance of maintaining an open mind. In the 19th century, the concept of germs causing diseases was not widely understood or accepted. In fact, many people at the time still believed that illnesses were the result of "bad air" or supernatural forces. It wasn't until Pasteur conducted his groundbreaking research that the scientific community began to recognize the existence of microorganisms and their role in causing diseases.

Pasteur's work began in 1854 when he was appointed professor of chemistry at the University of Lille. While there, he studied the process of fermentation, which ultimately led him to discover that microorganisms, such as bacteria and yeast, were responsible for the transformation of sugar into alcohol. This finding not only revolutionized the field of chemistry but also laid the groundwork for his later research on germ theory. In 1861, Pasteur published his findings, proving that bacteria were indeed the cause of many diseases. His research not only challenged the prevailing theories of the time but also opened the door for new approaches to medicine and public health.

As Pasteur's germ theory gained acceptance, it had a profound impact on the medical community and society at large. The discovery led to the development of antiseptic techniques in hospitals, which helped to drastically reduce the number of infections and deaths among patients. Additionally, Pasteur's work paved the way for the development of vaccines and other treatments that have saved countless lives over the years. It all began with his willingness to challenge conventional wisdom and explore new ideas, demonstrating the power of an open mind and the importance of embracing new possibilities.[4]

Victor leaned back in his chair, hands clasped on the back of his head, a thoughtful expression on his face. "Wow, I had no idea such a strategy even existed. How does the IRS view this?"

I reassured him, "The IRS recognizes this strategy, as long as you follow the rules and maintain proper documentation. It's completely legal and approved by the IRS. In fact, the Masters Exemption has its roots in the historical legislation related to the annual Masters Golf Tournament in Augusta, Georgia. Homeowners, to this day, rent out their homes to attendees and legally avoid paying any taxes on that income."

Victor seemed more excited now, shifting forward in his seat, the gears in his head turning as he thought of the potential savings. "What are some examples of business events that would qualify for this strategy?"

I offered a few ideas. "You could host a company retreat, employee training sessions, or even a client appreciation event at your home. Just make sure to keep records of the business purpose, the attendees, and the rental agreement between you and your business."

Victor nodded, taking it all in. "This could make a big differ-

---

[4] Agnes Ullman, "Louis Pasteur," Encyclopædia Britannica, April 27, 2023, https://www.britannica.com/biography/Louis-Pasteur#:~:text=Louis%20Pasteur%20is%20best%20known,preventing%20disease%20in%20silkworm%20eggs.

ence for me. Thank you for opening my eyes to this opportunity."

I smiled, happy to help. "You're welcome, Victor. It's always a pleasure to introduce clients to strategies they never knew existed. Remember, keeping an open mind can lead to powerful breakthroughs and significant savings."

With a newfound sense of optimism, Victor was ready to embrace the Masters Exemption and the potential tax savings it could provide. This was just one example of the many opportunities that can arise when we open our minds to new ideas and strategies.

As Jay Abraham once said, "As soon as you open your mind to doing things differently, the doors of opportunity practically fly off their hinges."[5] So, whether it's discovering the existence of germs or embracing tax-saving strategies like the Masters Exemption, keeping an open mind can lead to incredible growth and success. Don't let skepticism or fear of the unknown hold you back from exploring new opportunities that could change your life for the better.

The story of the *Miss Peregrine's Peculiar Children* series offers another powerful reminder of the importance of keeping an open mind. In the books, characters Enoch and Hugh scoff at the plausibility of a story from *Tales of the Peculiar*, dismissing it as ridiculous and impossible. However, Jacob reminds them

---

[5] "A Quote from the Sticking Point Solution," Goodreads, accessed June 19, 2023, https://www.goodreads.com/quotes/1135218-as-soon-as-you-open-your-mind-to-doing-things.

that just a few weeks earlier, he thought the same thing about the existence of people like them. This realization causes them to reconsider their stance and remain open to new ideas and possibilities.[6]

Similarly, Victor's initial skepticism about the Masters Exemption was replaced with an eagerness to learn more and apply the strategy to his own business. Once he understood the rules and saw the potential benefits, he realized that opportunities he had never considered before could be within his grasp.

Victor's experience with the Masters Exemption is a powerful testament to the value of seeking out and embracing new ideas and strategies. By opening his mind to the possibility of tax-saving strategies, Victor unlocked doors of opportunity that he never knew existed. It's a compelling reminder of the importance of approaching life with curiosity, flexibility, and an open mind.

As the examples of germ theory and the *Peculiar Children* series demonstrate, embracing an open-minded approach can lead to breakthroughs, improvements, and even life-changing discoveries. It certainly did for Victor! Don't let the unknown or skepticism hold you back. Explore new opportunities and strategies that could change your life for the better.

So, if you're a business owner like Victor or simply someone

---

[6] Paula Vince, "Why I Loved the 'Peculiar Children' Series," The Vince Review, June 22, 2017, https://vincereview.blogspot.com/2017/06/why-i-loved-peculiar-children-series.html.

looking to improve your financial situation, consider the possibilities that legal tax strategies could offer. Keep an open mind, explore your options, and you may be surprised by the doors of opportunity that fly open before you.

The Implementation

The Augusta Rule, also known as Section 280A(g) of the Internal Revenue Code, is a tax strategy that allows business owners to rent out their personal residence to their business for a limited number of days each year without having to report the rental income. Here is a step-by-step guide to implementing the Augusta Rule for business owners:

Step 1: Understand the requirements.

Before implementing the Augusta Rule, familiarize yourself with the requirements set forth in Section 280A(g). Key requirements include:

- The property must be rented for 14 days or fewer per year.

- The rental rate must be fair market value and not exceed the going rates for similar properties in the area.

Step 2: Consult a tax professional.

Consult a tax professional or accountant familiar with the Augusta Rule to determine if this strategy is suitable for your specific situation and to ensure compliance with IRS regulations.

Step 3: Establish a legitimate business purpose.

The use of your personal residence must serve a legitimate business purpose. Examples include hosting a business meeting, seminar, or training event. Document the purpose and agenda of the event to substantiate its business nature.

Step 4: Determine the fair market rental rate.

Research comparable properties in your area to determine a fair market rental rate for your residence. You may also consult a local real estate agent or appraiser to help establish an appropriate rate.

Step 5: Prepare a rental agreement.

Draft a formal rental agreement between you (as the homeowner) and your business, outlining the rental terms, including the rental rate, duration, and any other relevant terms. Both parties should sign the agreement.

Step 6: Host the business event.

Hold the planned business event at your residence, ensuring that it adheres to the legitimate business purpose stated in the rental agreement. Keep records of the event, such as invitations, attendee lists, and photographs.

Step 7: Issue payment for rent.

Your business should issue payments to you for the rent according to the terms of the rental agreement. Use a check or other traceable payment method to create a clear paper trail.

Step 8: Keep accurate records.

Maintain thorough records of the rental transactions, including the rental agreement, proof of payment, event documentation, and any other relevant documents. These records may be necessary to support your use of the Augusta Rule in case of an IRS audit.

Step 9: Tax reporting

Consult your tax professional to ensure proper reporting of the rental income and expenses on your tax returns. If you meet the requirements of Section 280A(g), you may not need to report the rental income on your personal tax return.[7]

Remember that tax laws and regulations can change, so always consult a tax professional to stay up-to-date on current rules and to ensure that you are compliant with IRS regulations.

---

[7] This can change depending on what type of entity you are using, so ensure you check with your CPA or Tax Strategist.

The Pitfalls

Here are some common pitfalls and areas where people may fail to meet the regulations for the Augusta Rule (Section 280A(g)) exclusion:

- Exceeding the 14-day limit: The property must be rented for 14 days or fewer per year. Renting it for more than 14 days will disqualify the income from the exclusion, and you will need to report the rental income on your tax return.

- Failing to establish a legitimate business purpose: The use of your personal residence must serve a legitimate business purpose. If you cannot prove that the rental served a genuine business purpose or if the event is merely a personal or social gathering, the IRS may disallow the exclusion.

- Charging an unreasonable rental rate: The rental rate must be consistent with the fair market value for similar properties in the area. Charging an inflated rental rate may raise red flags with the IRS and lead to the disallowance of the exclusion.

- Lack of proper documentation: It's crucial to maintain accurate records of the rental transactions, including the rental agreement, proof of payment, and event documentation. Insufficient or missing documentation could result in the IRS questioning the validity of the exclusion.

- Not reporting rental expenses correctly: If you claim rental expenses related to the use of your residence for business purposes, you may need to allocate those expenses between personal and rental use. Incorrect reporting of rental expenses could lead to disallowed deductions or adjustments to your taxable income.

- Mixing personal and business use: Ensure that the rented portion of your property is used solely for business purposes during the rental period. Mixing personal and business use could jeopardize the exclusion.

- Not consulting a tax professional: Failing to consult with a tax professional familiar with the Augusta Rule may result in errors in implementing the strategy or reporting the income and expenses on your tax returns. This could lead to potential issues with the IRS.

To avoid these pitfalls, ensure you comply with the regulations, maintain proper documentation, and consult with a tax professional to help navigate the complexities of the Augusta Rule.

Extreme Cases That Will Get You Thrown in Jail (Or Cause Otherwise Severe Penalties, Issues, or Problems for You!)

It's crucial to remember that the IRS pays close attention to unusual tax deductions or exclusions, especially those related to personal residences. To avoid potential issues, it's essential to strictly adhere to the requirements of Section 280A(g), maintain accurate records, and consult with a tax professional when implementing the Augusta Rule.

While there may not be any well-known cases involving abuses of the Augusta Rule, taxpayers should always be cautious when employing tax strategies and ensure they are following all IRS rules and regulations.

Some of the most common abuses that I have seen with taxpayers attempting to "get away" with bad things in regard to the Augusta Rule include:

1. Charging rents significantly above fair market value of rents: I had one case where the clients' CPA said that $50,000 per event was okay for a 2,000-square-foot house!

2. Not doing the research on the fair market value of rents: This was the same case as above. The CPA literally said in the IRS audit that he just "pulled the number out of thin air" and the client was forced to pay an almost $86,000 penalty!

3. Not documenting the business purpose: I had one client that had his assistant over to watch movies once a month and he was calling this the business purpose. Not quite what the IRS envisioned, a $7,000 penalty later ...

> Pigs get fat and hogs get slaughtered.
>
> —Mindy Jones, CPA[8]

---

[8] Mindy N Jones, CPA, was my favorite keynote speaker in my Masters of Taxation Graduate education program. This was one of her favorite sayings, and to this day I still use it. Rest in peace Mindy, you will never be forgotten!

If You Want to Know More (Bonus)

Unlock the potential of the Masters Exemption/Augusta Rule with our comprehensive PDF guide. This tax strategy can provide you with incredible opportunities and substantial savings.

Our PDF delves deep into the details of the Masters Exemption/Augusta Rule, explaining how it allows you to leverage your home(s) and qualifying properties for significant tax benefits.

By downloading our PDF, you'll gain access to expert insights, key eligibility criteria, and practical examples to help you make the most of the Masters Exemption/Augusta Rule. Learn how to navigate the intricacies of this tax strategy, ensuring compliance while maximizing your tax savings.

Don't miss out on the chance to turn your home into an even more valuable tax advantage. Visit our website to download the PDF and embark on your journey toward tax savings:

TaxGoddess.com/14Days

If you need further guidance or have specific questions about implementing the Masters Exemption/Augusta Rule, our team of specialists is here to assist you. We have extensive experience in this area and can provide tailored support to help you capitalize on this unique tax strategy.

Since this strategy should be implemented within a comprehensive plan, the provided details are generally applicable and may not cover all circumstances.

Tying it all Together

This book has aimed to provide valuable insights, strategies, and real-life examples of how to achieve The 6% Life—a life where taxes are minimized, financial freedom is attainable, and businesses can flourish.

We have explored various tax strategies, such as the DB Plans, Paying Your Kids, Accountable Plans, Infinite Banking, and the Masters Exemption, as well as the importance of having a solid team behind every business owner to ensure proper implementation and guidance.

As you reflect on the lessons and principles shared throughout this book, we want to extend an open invitation for you to reach out to our team and discuss the strategies presented here.

We understand that each business and individual has unique needs and circumstances, and we are committed to helping you find the best solutions tailored to your specific situation. Our team is well-equipped to provide you with additional strategies and support that can empower you to achieve your own version of The 6% Life.

Remember that the journey to financial freedom and success is not a solitary one. It requires a collaborative effort, open communication, and the unwavering commitment of a dedicated team. We, at Tax Goddess, are here to support you in realizing your dreams and ambitions.

Together, we can build a strong foundation for your financial future, allowing you to focus on growing your business, enjoying life, and making a lasting impact in your industry.

Thank you for joining us on this journey through the world of tax strategies and business success.

We hope that the knowledge and stories shared within these pages have inspired and motivated you to take control of your financial destiny.

If you're ready to embark on the path to The 6% Life, don't hesitate to reach out to us.

I look forward to partnering with you and helping you achieve your goals.

—Shauna A. Wekherlien, CPA, MTax, CTC, CTS, the Tax Goddess

PART III
How to Get Even More Help

Your Golden Ticket to The 6% Life

I firmly believe that empowering business owners with financial acumen is the cornerstone of a thriving economy.

It's not just about making more money—it's about keeping it where it matters: in the hands of innovative, driven individuals like you. I'm committed to ensuring you don't part with a penny more than the bare legal minimum when it comes to taxes.

I'm thrilled to offer you a complimentary one-month access to our exclusive coaching program, The 6% Life. This program is our treasure trove of financial wisdom, and I want you to experience its benefits firsthand.

But what does it mean to live The 6% Life? It's about embodying a unique perspective where taxes are not a burden but a tool. A tool that can be wielded skillfully to carve your path to financial freedom and success.

The 6% Life coaching program is your guide to mastering the art of tax strategy. We delve deeper into a variety of tax strategies, helping business owners and entrepreneurs while providing clarity and actionable steps. You'll have access to one month of our live Q&A sessions with our exclusive community of like-minded entrepreneurs and business owners.

So, how do you start your journey into The 6% Life? Visit **TaxGoddess.com/SixLife** and use code: **61BOOK** to redeem your free one-month access. But don't wait too long, because the tax clock is always ticking, and every moment is an opportunity for savings.

I'm excited to welcome you into our community of savvy tax strategists.

How to Access Your Bonuses

Sprinkled throughout this book are several free bonuses. They are training videos posted on our website to accompany the contents of this book.

You'll see the links to the videos included throughout the chapters, and I've included this list of each one for quick reference.

1. Aggression Scale training:

    TaxGoddess.com/AggressionScale

2. 831(b) program details:

    TaxGoddess.com/831b

3. Pay My Kids:

    TaxGoddess.com/PayMyKids

4. DST Webinar: **DST4Me.com**

5. Accountable plan document:

    bit.ly/AcctPlanDoc

6. Income and expense tracker:

    TaxGoddess.com/Income-Expense-Tracker

7. Accountable plan calculation:

   TaxGoddess.com/Accountable-Plan-Calculation-Tool

8. Infinite Banking Guide:

   TaxGoddess.com/IBTactics

9. Masters Exemption Guide:

   TaxGoddess.com/14Days

10. One month access to The 6% Life Group Coaching Program:

    a. Visit **TaxGoddess.com/SixLife**

    b. Use code **61BOOK** to redeem your free one-month access.

Speak to Us

If you've read all of this and are in overwhelm and just want a professional to take care of it all or just want to have someone ensure you aren't leaving thousands in the hands of the IRS, I would like to invite you to speak to us.

Head over to **TaxGoddess.com/Growth-Team**.

You can book an appointment online to speak with one of my team members. You will be sent a short questionnaire asking a few questions about your business and personal financial world (so that we can review them before the call).

Answer the questions, submit your tax documentation as requested, and then meet with our team member.

On the first call, my office will review some of the details with you—a short call—just to make sure we know the big picture.

Our team will then review in depth the files you've sent over and identify problems and missed opportunities to see if and by how much in tax savings we can help.

If we can help, we will show you what it looks like to work with us. This includes how much you can save, what working with us is like, how our programs work, and how much it would cost.

You can then decide if you want to become one of our clients. No pressure, but either way, you will get a lot of clarity from this call.

Visit TaxGoddess.com/Growth-Team to book your call today. We can't wait to speak with you!

Acknowledgments

I want to thank all of the people who helped me make this book, and my dream life, a reality.

Thank you to Christa—my main source of inspiration for almost everything I do. For always believing in me, telling me that I am smart, pretty, talented, and capable of absolutely anything I ever wanted.

Thank you to my constant team of support—Rajendra, Tanushree, and Shubham. You bought me the time I needed to write this book that will help hundreds of thousands of business owners out there keep their money in their pocket. Without your dedication to the detailed work of the cause, I would have never had time to be able to write this book in the first place.

Thank you to those who keep me on track and handle my life, so my brain can focus on what needs to be done—Michael, Chetan, MD, Ankur, Ramesh, Shreeya, Yusuf, Ankur, Mia, Sophia, and Yadwinder.

Thank you to Fred K. for always being the voice inside my head, telling me "Do or do not, there is no try," and "Hope is NOT a strategy."

Thanks to Alex L. for the constant "atta girls" and his never-ending faith and guidance.

About the Author

Shauna A. Wekherlien, CPA, MTax, CTC, CTS, is a U.S. Top 1% ranked, highly sought-after Tax Strategist. She is passionate about helping successful business owners, entrepreneurs, and high-wage earners reduce their tax burden. Having founded Tax Goddess Business Services, PC, in 2004, she has built a large global team of tax specialists who use "plain language" (not tax code) to help her clients create tax opportunities and manage tax risk legally.

Shauna, the "Tax Goddess" as she's fondly called, is engaging and enthusiastic and has been called a "pure joy" to work with.

She makes taxes "fun." Her proprietary program, STC (Strategic Tax Coaching), boasts a current average tax rate of 6.92% for her clients. With over 4,700 tax plans written thus far, the Tax Goddess team has been able to help clients save over $1 billion in taxes.

Shauna herself is a zealous tax and financial educator. She is a highly demanded author and speaker with advanced communication and public speaking skills. Over the past 24 years, she has been featured in many magazines such as *Forbes* and *Entrepreneur*, as well as hundreds of television and podcast appearances such as *CNN, CBS, NBC*, the *10 Minute Entrepreneur*, the *LifeBlood Podcast*, and the *Action and Ambition Podcast*.

Shauna A. Wekherlien, CPA's background is in:

- High Wealth Financial Planning Management (KPMG),

- Business tax strategy and planning (American Express—Tax & Business Services), and

- Wealth transfer and business entity strategy

Her areas of expertise include:

- Tax structuring via entity management (How to set up, deal with, and operate S-Corps, Partnerships, Sole Proprietorships, and C-Corps)

ABOUT THE AUTHOR

- Cash flow/entity fund management (making sure your bottom line is as high as possible)

- Real estate transactions (foreclosures, short sales, investing, fix and flips, Real Estate Professional Status)

- LLC management (determining how to move money between entities for the minimum tax owed or largest refund possible!)

She speaks a little bit of Spanish, loves to travel, and has four dogs: Shade (the old man), Eos (the destroyer of water sprinklers!), Thor (her Big Boy), and Cato (the serious) who are her favorite little "monsters."

www.ingramcontent.com/pod-product-compliance
Lightning Source LLC
Chambersburg PA
CBHW070424010526
44118CB00014B/1896